Our Nation Under God

Michael J. McHugh

Arlington Heights, Illinois
Christian Liberty Press

A publication of
Christian Liberty Press
502 West Euclid Avenue
Arlington Heights, Illinois 60004

Scripture references are conformed to The Holy Bible, New King James Version ©1982, Thomas Nelson, Inc., so that modern readers may gain greater comprehension of the Word of God.

Written by McHugh, Michael J.

OUR NATION UNDER GOD
Includes index
1. History–Juvenile literature
2. Social Studies–Juvenile literature

Copyediting by Diane C. Olson
Layout by Edward J. Shewan

ISBN 978-1-930092-87-7
      1-930092-87-3

Printed in the United States of America

Preface

Young students often struggle to comprehend the flow of history in general and the origins of American history in particular. The text that follows has been designed to help youngsters obtain a fundamental understanding of how the nations of the earth developed and why the Americas were among the last continents to be settled. This book also provides a simple overview of the history of the United States and its geography.

In addition to these features, the text seeks to give students a clearer grasp of God's purposes for civil government, family government, church government, and self-government. It is the author's desire to do more than simply tell students the way things are in the world. Youngsters need to be told why our world is the way it is. In short, they need to be given a basic framework for understanding God's plan for the world He has made.

May the mighty God of heaven and earth bless those students who study this history text.

—*Michael J. McHugh*

Contents

The lighthouse shines forth its light to safely guide ships into the harbor. In the same way, the light from God's Word can guide students into a clearer understanding of history.

1 God Governs Everything

In the beginning God created the heavens and the earth.—Genesis 1:1

The Bible teaches us that Jesus Christ made everything and everyone in the world. He made the land and sea. He made each person who walks on the earth.

Every man, woman, and child, therefore, has the duty to serve and glorify the great Creator God. The same God who made each of us also controls the world He has created. God controls the creatures that He made through the laws that He has given them in the Holy Bible. He also controls the life of each person through God the Holy Spirit.

God Rules the World

God's control over the world is called His government. The mighty Creator expects each person to follow His rules for living so they can be holy and happy. Unless we follow God's Law, we will not know how to serve and glorify our Maker. When the people of the world honor God's gov-

"The earth is the Lord's, and all its fullness..." (Psalm 24:1a). God created the earth and all creatures to bring glory to Himself.

ernment, they enjoy peace on earth. When people refuse to follow God's plan, they find only sadness and death. We will now learn about the four types of governments that God set up to rule mankind.

God's Plan Has Four Kinds of Government

1.	**SELF-GOVERNMENT** **(A plan for each person)**
2.	**FAMILY GOVERNMENT** **(A plan for the family)**
3.	**CHURCH GOVERNMENT** **(A plan for the church)**
4.	**CIVIL GOVERNMENT** **(A plan for each nation)**

God rules over each nation with the heavenly light of His wisdom and power.

Self-government— God's Plan for Each Person

When God made Adam and Eve, He gave them rules or laws to follow. However, the first man and woman chose to break the rules God had made because they thought that they could live by their own wisdom. They did not want to obey God and live under His loving rule of government.

After Adam and Eve sinned, they lost the ability to follow God and His Word. All of mankind fell into the paths of sin and rebellion set by Adam and Eve. For this reason, everyone is a slave to the sinful nature that seeks to follow the wisdom of men instead of the wisdom of God.

In the Bible we read:

> **Man shall not live by bread alone, but by every word that proceeds from the mouth of God.—Matthew 4:4**

This Bible verse teaches that all people on earth have the duty to live their lives according to the teachings of the Word of God. Sometimes this is called the duty of self-government under God's Law. All boys and girls must build their lives around the truths that God has given in the Bible.

Children must ask the Lord to give them hearts that want to obey His commandments. When God gives people the power to cheerfully obey, they can begin to practice self-control or self-government.

Even a child is known by his deeds, by whether what he does is pure and right. Proverbs 20:11

■ Exercise

9-29-15

List five things you can do to be self-governed under God's Law.

w/ Mom

1.	*Tell the truth*
2.	*Obey my Mom and Dad*

3.	Don't hit in anger.
4.	Be wise with my time.
5.	Don't take what is not mine.

A good child will want to be self-controlled or self-governed under God's Law. Unless a person is brought to the point where he can follow God's ways without having to be forced, he will never be able to live peaceably with any of God's governments.

Self-government, therefore, is the most basic and important type of government in God's plan for mankind. Wicked people by their very nature will not be controlled by God's Law and will be unable to live happy and fruitful lives. In the book of First Corinthians we read: "But the natural man does not receive the things of the Spirit of God, for they are foolishness unto him; nor can he know them, because they are spiritually discerned" (1 Corinthians 2:14).

The power to turn away from sin comes from God. Only by trusting in the work of Jesus Christ as Savior can a sinner find the strength to live a godly life.

To understand why people need to obey God's rules, we can think about a baseball game. If there were no rules in a baseball game, and every player and team did something different, there would be no game. And if each player tried to be the coach and refused to stay in his position, the team would fall apart.

In the same way, God controls the world and sets the rules for the game of life. People who refuse to follow God's rules will find that their lives fall apart. The Lord has a perfect order and plan for mankind to follow. The Word of God, the Bible, shows us God's rules for living.

Without rules and order, a baseball game would be impossible to play.

Family Government— God's Plan for the Family

The Bible teaches us that after God made Adam, He said that it was not good for man to be alone. The wise Creator decided to make a special helper for Adam so he would be completely happy and not lonely. When God created Eve and brought her to Adam, He made the first family!

Before Adam and Eve sinned, they lived together in perfect unity and happiness. God planned for the government of the family to protect and bless them. He also planned for Adam and Eve to take responsibility for the care and spiritual nurturing of the children that God would send.

After Adam and Eve sinned, God's plan for the family was still the same. Men and women, however, would not be able to live together in perfect peace and joy because of sin.

God, in His wisdom, had already chosen the man to be the head of his family. Nevertheless, the family would now need a strong leader to keep peace in the household. The father would be responsible to see that God's loving commands were followed by each family member. The wife would help her husband and submit to his leadership as long as it was not wicked. Children would have the duty to honor and obey their parents for the Lord's sake. Special

The family is designed by God to be the basic unit of society.

blessings were promised for children who honored their parents.

> **Honor your father and your mother, that your days may be long upon the land which the Lord your God is giving you.**
> **—Exodus 20:12**

The government of the family became even more necessary to men, women, and children after sin entered the world. The world became deceived by Satan and his lies. People began to hurt and hate one another as they followed the foolish ways of Satan. The family unit provided children with the important blessings of loving support and protection, as well as companionship and education.

The wise Creator knew how important the government of the family would be as He planned the best way for people to live together. Many children do not enjoy the blessing of a loving home with caring parents. In such cases, God Himself is able to care for children who turn to Him as their heavenly Father.

Families should be places of loving support and protection.

10 – 7 – 15

■ Activity

Complete the family tree on the page below by filling in the names of your family members. Feel free to ask your parents for help with this project.

Leslie Eugene Feldick
GRANDFATHER

Larry Wesley Gardner
GRANDFATHER

Iris Kathaleen (Gray) Feldick
GRANDMOTHER

LaRita Mae (Stalter) Gardner
GRANDMOTHER

Todd Leslie Feldick
FATHER

Kimberly Renee Feldick
MOTHER

Daniel Gray Feldick
YOUR NAME

Father

Mother

If God has blessed you with a family, please draw pictures of your parents in the top boxes or glue in photographs of them.

Do you have brothers or sisters? If so, please draw pictures of them in the boxes below or glue in photographs of them.

Brother or Sister

Brother or Sister

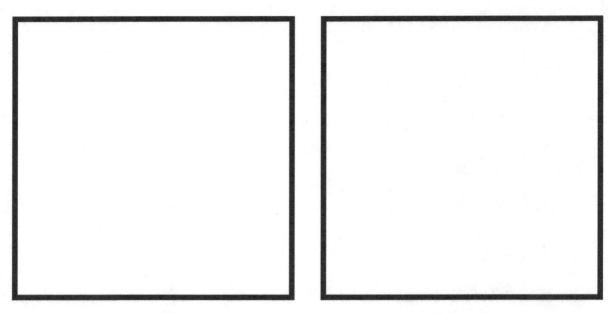

Grandfather   **Grandmother**

Do you know who your grandparents are? Your grandparents are your parents' moms and dads! Draw pictures of two of them, if possible, in the boxes above or glue in photographs of two of your grandparents.

Church Government—God's Plan for the Church

Since the days of Adam and Eve, God has always had people to worship and serve Him. Today every person, young or old, who loves God is a part of His Church. People sometimes make the mistake of thinking that the Church is a building of some kind. The true Church, however, is made up of people who trust in and serve the God of the Bible.

It has always been God's plan that man bring glory to his Creator. After man's fall into sin, however, it became important for man to be under the direction of spiritual leaders in the Church. Before man's fall, he did not need anyone to help him worship and serve God. After the Fall, it became very important for man to submit to God's plan for helping him to grow in the knowledge and grace of Jesus Christ. This is why God gave His people Church government.

In the days since Jesus Christ died and rose again, the Church of Jesus Christ has grown from a tiny group of teachers and disciples to a large number of people throughout the world. Like any other government, the Church has men in places of leadership. God Himself calls men to serve the Church as pastors or elders. These leaders have the special duty to teach the Bible faithfully and administer the sacraments of baptism and the Lord's Supper. The Lord has also given the Church deacons. These men take special care of the physical needs of church families as well as the practical needs of the church building.

One of the primary duties of Church government is to make sure that God's people are being equipped to stand against Satan and his kingdom of darkness. In the Bible, God promises to build His Church so that Satan and wicked people shall not overcome it. Jesus Christ, the true head of the Church, once said: "I will build my church, and the gates of hell shall not prevail against it" (Matthew 6:18b).

Our faith in God is supported and nourished by the work of Church leaders who are themselves faithful to the Word of God. We should be willing to give respect and honor to Church leaders who stand firmly for Christ and His Word.

■ Activity   10-8-15

What is the name of your church?
Lakeside Baptist

Who are your church leaders? **Pastors'/Elders' names:**
Pastor Chuck Ells
Earl Tekippe , Mark Ingram

Deacons' names:
Earl Granroth
Mike Granlund

Obey those who rule over you, and be submissive, for they watch out for your souls, as those who must give account. Let them do so with joy and not with grief, for that would be unprofitable for you.—Hebrews 13:17

Civil Government—God's Plan for the Nations

Before Adam and Eve sinned, they were able to practice perfect self-government by God's grace. They always did what they were told to do, just as God commanded. After our first parents rebelled against their Maker, however, they no longer were naturally good. Obeying God from the heart became impossible for Adam and Eve and all their children after them. They chose to live their lives apart from God's Law and government. They loved darkness and sin more than their Creator.

God gives judges the duty to punish evildoers and protect innocent people.

In the days of Noah, men were so wicked that God destroyed most of them with a great flood. Afterward, He gave this command: "Whoever sheds man's blood, by man his blood shall be shed…" (Genesis 9:6a). This established the foundation of civil government.

God in His mercy planned for a special government called civil government to enforce God's Law throughout the nations of the earth. God knew that unless there were rulers who were given power to punish people who

were doing evil acts against their neighbors, the world would soon be like hell itself. Civil government leaders such as presidents or kings, governors, city leaders, and judges have the duty to protect people by punishing those who do evil acts.

All of us have the duty to obey the laws that our civil leaders make, unless such laws clearly go against God's Law. When we follow rules for living made by faithful leaders in civil government, we are honoring the will or plan of God for our lives. The Bible states: "Submit yourselves to every ordinance of man for the Lord's sake, whether to the king … or to governors" (1 Peter 2:13, 14).

Policemen help keep our cities peaceful. They carry guns by God's authority for this purpose.

Without the help of civil government leaders, our cities, towns, and nations would soon be controlled by wicked men who would spread death and sadness. For this reason, God's Law gives great power to civil leaders to punish criminals and lawbreakers.

For example, God has given such leaders the power to kill criminals who wrongfully take the lives of other human beings. Because of this punishment, wicked murderers are discouraged from taking the lives of good people and are forced to live peaceably.

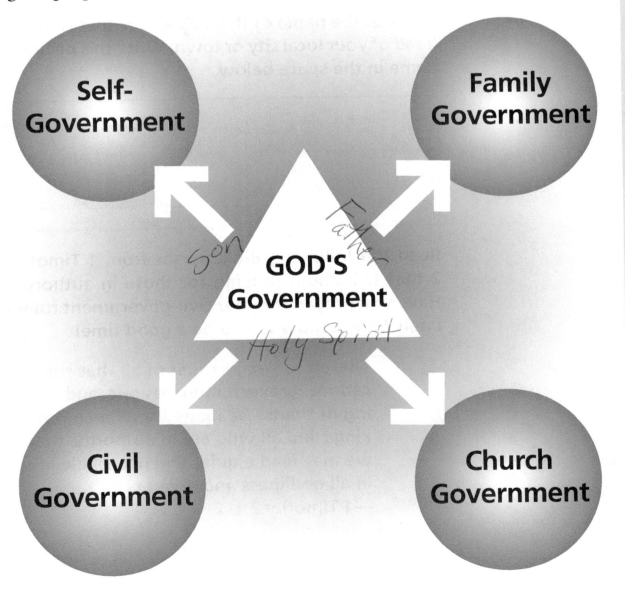

Four Governments Under God

Our wise and wonderful Creator gave mankind four great governments to enable human beings to live together in peace. The goodness and wisdom of God can be seen in His plan to set up godly governments for people to follow. We must all do our part to submit to God's will for ourselves, our families, our churches, and our civil institutions.

■ Activity   *10-19-15*

Find out the name of the civil leader that is at the head of your local city or town. Write this person's name in the space below.

Governor of state

Scott   Walker
(good man)

Read the following Bible verses from 1 Timothy 2 that talk about praying for those in authority. Have you prayed for your civil-government rulers lately? If not, now would be a good time!

> Therefore I exhort first of all that supplications, prayers, intercessions, and giving of thanks be made for all men, for kings and all who are in authority, that we may lead a quiet and peaceable life in all godliness and reverence.
> —1 Timothy 2:1, 2

Make up a special prayer list for civil leaders in your part of the country and use this listing as a reminder to pray each week for civil leaders.

1. _____
_____

2. _____
_____

3. _____
_____

4. _____
_____

5. _____
_____

6. _____
_____

7. _____
_____

8. _____
_____

9. _____
_____

10. _____
_____

10-22-15

Chapter 1 Review

Fill in the blanks with the correct answers.

1. God rules the world He made through __*4*__ special governments.

2. __*Self*__ government lets a person follow God's Law without having to be forced.

3. __*Family*__ government gives human beings the blessings of loving support and protection, as well as companionship and education.

4. __*Church*__ government helps God-fearing people to strengthen their faith and to stand against Satan.

5. __*Civil*__ government has been given the power to force people to live by the laws of God and to punish evildoers.

6. What Bible verse tells us to pray for our leaders? _____

    _____

The first people to travel to North America sometimes built their homes in the rocky areas around mountain ranges.

2 God Made the Nations

He has made from one blood every nation of men to dwell on all the face of the earth, and has determined their preappointed times and the boundaries of their habitation, so that they should seek the Lord....
—Acts 17:26, 27a

After the days of Adam and Eve, the people of the earth began to grow more and more wicked. As the years passed, God saw that His creatures had become so filled with foolishness that they would never submit to His rule of law or government. God warned the people through His faithful servant Noah that He would destroy the earth with a flood unless the people turned away from sin. The people, however, did not listen to God and were destroyed in a great worldwide flood. Only Noah and his family were saved because they built a huge boat, or ark, as God had commanded.

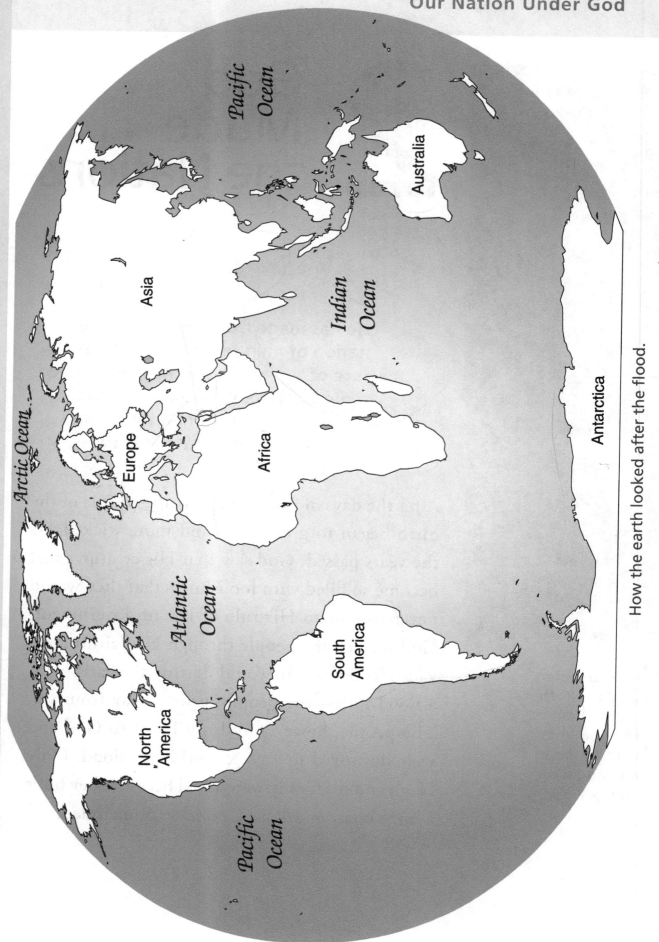

How the earth looked after the flood.

God Formed the Continents

After the flood, Noah and his family left the ark. The earth that they walked on had changed a great deal during the great flood. First of all, the earth now had huge areas of water on it called oceans. As you can see on the map on the previous page, the world has more water on it than land. If you study the map, you will see that there are four big oceans.

The land also changed. The surface of the earth was broken up by the powerful flood. Huge mountains and deep valleys were formed all over the earth. The great area of dry land was changed by God and divided into seven large pieces. These large pieces of land are called continents.

With your teacher's help, locate the seven continents and the four oceans on the map of the world. Memorize the name of each continent and ocean and write their names in the spaces below.

10-22-15

CONTINENTS	OCEANS
1. North America	1. Pacific
2. South America	2. Atlantic
3. Africa	3. Indian
4. Europe	4. Pacific
5. Antarctica	
6. Australia	
7. Asia	

The Tower of Babel

God would not bless the people who began to build the Tower of Babel.

After the days of Noah, the people of the earth were still not willing to live at peace with God. Over time, the families of the earth began to live together in large groups called tribes. These people joined together in the land where the nation of Iraq is now located. The leaders decided to build a huge tower that would reach up to heaven. They refused to follow God's command for them to move away into other parts of the earth and fill it. God, however, was able to get these people to obey His command in an interesting way.

One day, as these people were building their tower, the Lord changed the language, or speech, of the tribes. Suddenly, the people began to become confused because the different groups of people were speaking in new and strange languages. Because they could not understand each other, they were not able to keep building the tower. They were forced to move away and settle in different areas around the world.

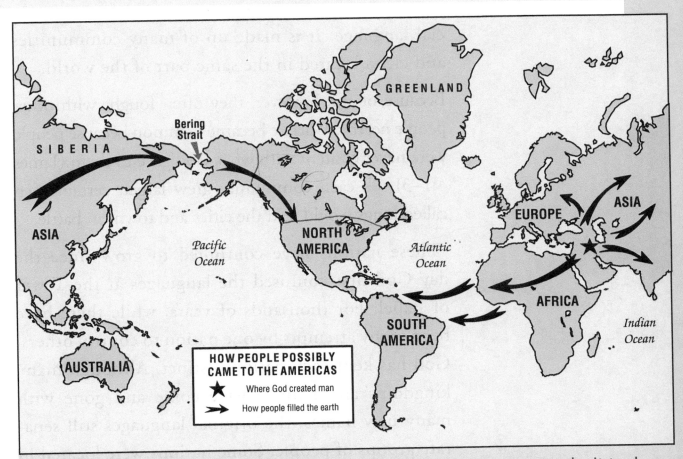

This map shows us how groups of people filled the earth. Can you see why it took so long for people to walk or sail to the Americas?

The wise Creator wanted the people to be scattered throughout the earth, with different languages, so that no one group of wicked people would have too much power. As the Lord forced people to move into new lands and set up new communities, He formed the nations.

As these groups moved from one part of the earth to the next, they looked for good locations in which to live. Often these places had natural borders such as rivers, mountains, valleys, and oceans. Over time, as their communities developed, they built towns and cities. Each nation is set apart by its own special language. It is made up of many communities and cities located in the same part of the world.

Because of sin, however, they often fought with other people nearby. Warfare became common because people were never content with what God gave to them (James 4:1–3). As each community grew larger, certain men called kings would lead the cities and towns in battle.

These nations have continued to grow since the day God first confused the languages at the Tower of Babel. For thousands of years, while there have been many attempts by one nation to control others, God has kept each nation distinct. Although many kingdoms and nations have come and gone with many new names, the original languages still separate groups of people. Some nations were located in very small land areas, while others were very large and highly developed. This was because some people groups had many children, while others had few. God also destroyed many nations in His judgments.

The Nations Settle the Earth

Have you ever wondered what areas of the world were first explored by people as they set up communities and nations? The Bible and other old writings and maps help us to understand the answer to this question.

The three sons of Noah led the early tribes of people to the area around the Tower of Babel in modern-day Iraq. These men were named Shem, Ham, and Japheth.

The sons and daughters of these men, and their families who traveled with them, were the people whom God forced out of the area near the Tower of Babel. Most of the children, or descendants, of Noah began to move away from the Middle East in all directions. Some moved north into the continent of Asia. Some traveled north into Europe. Other groups went south into the continent of Africa. A few of the descendants of Noah built their homes and cities in the Middle East itself.

People Travel to North America

When, you may ask, did the different groups of people start to move into the continent of North America? That is not a very easy question to answer. One thing is for certain: it took many hundreds of years for any human being to travel to the North American continent. Why do you suppose this was the case? Let's look

The American Indians often used animals to help them move from place to place.

again at the map of the world on page 23, with its seven continents, and see why it took so long for the people of the world to visit North or South America.

The truth is, we have very few written records of the people who first set foot on North America. For this reason, we do not know exactly how these early explorers got to America. And we do not know what tribe or nation these people came from.

Most historians think that people who lived in north-west Africa and Asia were the first ones to come to the Americas. As shown in the previous map, it is believed that people from Africa sailed first to South America with boats or big rafts and then walked up into North America. The people from Asia, it is believed, were able to walk across a land bridge that once connected Asia to North America over the Bering Strait.

Does the continent of North America look familiar to you? It should, if you live in the United States,

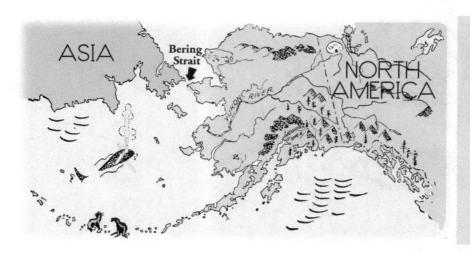

The first people to travel to North America probably went over a land bridge at the Bering Strait.

Long ago animals such as bison roamed wild and free over North America.

for the nation called the United States now fills up much of the continent.

Young students should understand, however, that it took a long, long time for groups of people to settle in North and South America. God decided to let people first settle in other parts of the world in the days of long ago. So people began to slowly move throughout Asia, Africa, Europe, and the Middle East. Over time,

The early Americans always had plenty of deer to hunt. Indian children often had clothes made out of deerskin.

little and big cities began to spring up in these parts of the world. As for the Americas, God simply kept these two big continents a secret for many years.

The American Indians

For thousands of years, only wild animals and a few brave explorers lived on the huge lands in North and South America. However, several hundred years before Jesus Christ was born in Bethlehem, groups of people began to form small tribes in parts of the Americas. These people came to be called Indians by those men who explored the American continents in later years. It is more proper, however, simply to say that these people were the first Americans.

The first Americans were a clever people who lived in small tents or huts in the forest. They hunted animals and farmed the land to feed their families. Their clothes were often made of deerskin or perhaps the fur from a bear.

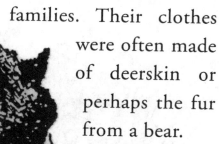

Bears loved to walk in the big forests of North America.

Indian warriors loved to shoot their arrows.

The Indian leaders did not think it was important to build schools, libraries, cities, or churches. They spent much of their time hunting, making things they needed in order to live, or fighting with each other. So-called medicine men, or witch doctors, filled these people's lives with strange and ungodly customs and laws. For these and other reasons, the first people in

The first Americans were skilled hunters.

America made little forward progress in building a great nation.

This map shows the three nations that make up North America today.

It is very likely that the first Americans came from one of the ancient tribes that was forced away from the Tower of Babel around 4000 B.C.

They became so cut off from the God-fearing tribes that they lost the knowledge of the true God. In any case, we do know that the first Americans had somehow lost the knowledge of the Lord and were living in the darkness of sin. Almighty God, however, would send explorers to the New World of America in later years to give the Indian people the knowledge of Jesus Christ and His Word.

The first Americans lived in simple homes. Some Indians liked to live in movable tents called teepees.

Indians who lived in the Southwest built their homes in rocky areas near mountains.

11-19-15

Chapter 2 Review

Fill in the blanks with the correct answers.

orally

Fantastic!!

1. After the days of Noah, wicked people came together and started to build a _____tower_____.

2. God forced these wicked people to move away to different places in the earth by changing their _____language_____.

3. The Lord does not want any one group of sinful people to have too much _____power_____.

4. A _____nation_____ is made up of many communities and cities located in the same part of the world.

5. The first nations on earth were set up in the _Middle_ East.

6. Many nations were also set up in Asia and _Europe_ in the days after the Tower of Babel.

7. God simply kept the two big continents of _North_ America and _South_ America a secret for many years.

8. The first Americans were called _____Indians_____ by the explorers from Europe.

3 The Period of Discovery

Sailing ships like those pictured above were used by explorers to find new lands.

To everything there is a season, a time for every purpose under heaven. —Ecclesiastes 3:1

To help us understand the exact time that God worked out His plan for the world in past days, we use dates. Without dates, it would be very hard to know which events came first and which followed.

Dates Help Us See God's Plans

Dates are often written down by the month and the day and the year. Most children know the month and day of their birthday—do you? See if you can find out the year in which you were born as well.

There is a birthday that we honor in a special way for a special person. That person is Jesus Christ, who is the Son of God. The birth of Christ is the most important date in history. For this reason, we give or list dates based upon the birthday of Jesus Christ. The birthday of Christ is the starting point. Every date "before Christ" was born is called "B.C.," and the years B.C. count down to the year zero—about when Jesus was born. If we say that God scattered the tribes of the earth at Babel in the year 4000 B.C., we mean it happened 4,000 years before Jesus was born. Every date after Jesus' birth is called A.D., and the years A.D. go up from zero. A.D. stands for the words "anno Domini," which means "in the year of our Lord." If you were born in the year A.D. 2003, that means you were born 2,003 years after Jesus was born. The Pilgrims landed at Plymouth in A.D. 1620, or 1,620 years after Jesus was born. If a date does not say B.C. next to it, it usually means A.D.

As we have already noted, the large continent of North America had very few people living on it in the days of long ago. Even the Indian tribes had little contact with each other because they were far apart. We must also remember that North America had no roads, no cars, trains, or airplanes at this time in history. Therefore, it took a long time for people to travel from place to place. The next map will show you where most of the Indian tribes in eastern North America were located around the year 1500.

The Vikings

The people who lived on the continent of Europe were among the first to send out explorers to far-away lands. A bold and daring tribe from the land of Scandinavia known as the "Vikings," or "North-men," were great adventurers. Around the year 1000, groups of Viking ships set sail across the wide Atlantic Ocean in search of new lands. Their leader was a man named Leif Ericson.

These brave sailors discovered the lands of Iceland and Greenland around the year 1000. A short time later, they continued to sail farther across the Atlan-

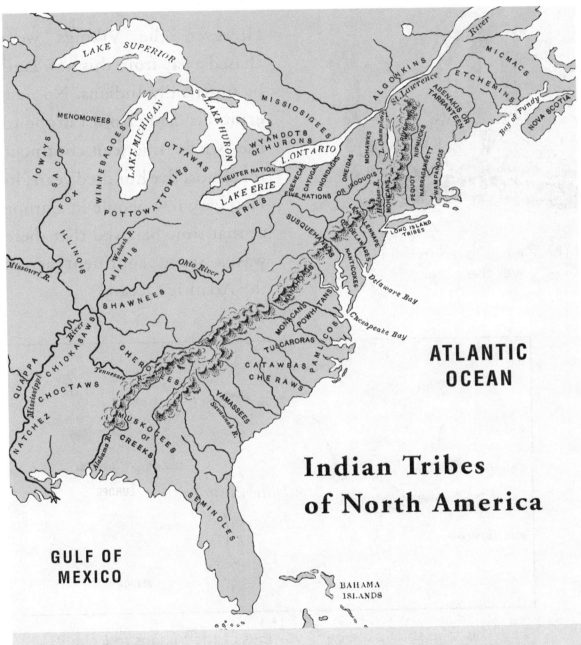

Early Indian groups or tribes in the eastern part of North America

tic Ocean until they landed in parts of modern-day Canada and New England. The Vikings had reached North America from Europe! They called this new land "Vineland," because they found huge grapes growing in parts of the land they explored.

However, the Vikings were chased away from this new land by unfriendly Indians. No new explorers came from Europe to the North American continent for almost five hundred years. In fact, very few people in Europe at that time believed that there was a secret continent across the Atlantic Ocean.

The Vikings loved to sail far over the oceans.

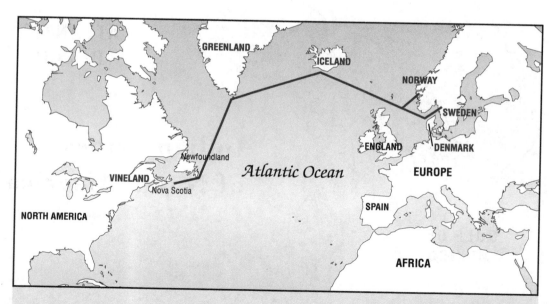

This map shows the early voyages of the Vikings to Iceland, Greenland, and Vineland.

The continents of the earth that God did permit people to settle in began to fill up with more people and more cities. Large and beautiful cities were filled with busy people trying to improve their way of life. People could travel from place to place faster than in earlier years because of better roads and great inventions like the horse-drawn cart. Still, sailing ships were often used to move important and heavy things like food, clothing, and gold from one nation of the world to another. Ships could sail across the water much faster than an ox or horse could walk things from place to place.

Explorers from Europe

During the 1400s, many people in Europe were trying to find a faster and better way to travel to Asia and other parts of the known world. More and more people wanted to trade things with people who lived far away. However, they did not want to have to walk half-way around the world to

When Columbus was a boy, he loved to watch the big ships.

pick up or drop off things. If only someone could find a better way to travel from Europe to Asia!

Columbus and his crew took three ships to the New World. The ships were called the *Niña*, *Pinta*, and *Santa Maria*.

Finally, in 1492 an explorer from Europe named Christopher Columbus was able to sail from Spain to the Americas. This brave sailor thought that he could reach a part of Asia by sailing west across the Atlantic Ocean. In fact, Columbus sailed to the New World four times and never knew that he had rediscovered America! He thought that he had found a quicker way to reach the part of Asia known as the East Indies. This is why Columbus made the mistake of naming the people he discovered "Indians."

It was the Lord who put it into my mind ... the fact that it would be possible to sail from here to the Indies ... the fact that the Gospel must be preached to so many lands in such a short time—this is what convinces me.
—Christopher Columbus

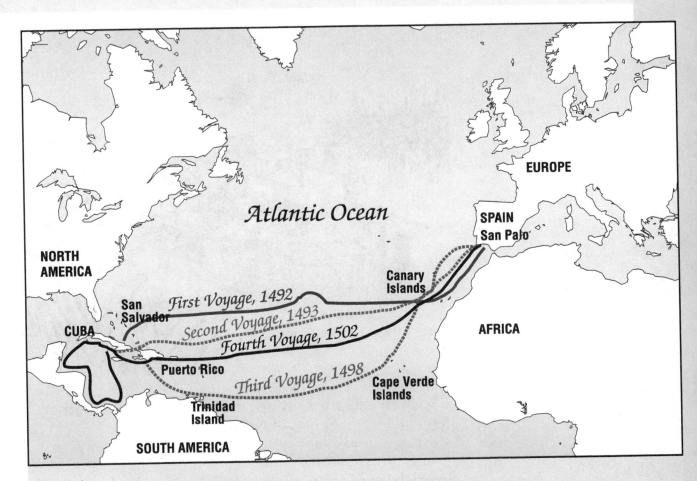

Columbus made four trips to the Americas.

Spanish Explorers

In the years following the adventures of Columbus, many more Spanish explorers came to the Americas. These sailors discovered many lands and people in South America and Central America. They also made the first European settlement in North America in the state we now call Florida. The first city to be built in North America was called St. Augustine. This Spanish town was built in the year 1565.

Spanish explorers set up cities in Florida and in other parts of North America.

Spanish explorers traveled into North America in many directions. Many of these explorers visited the southwestern and far western parts of North America.

The Spanish set up cities and mission stations as far west as the California territory. They also brought horses to the New World to travel on and to trade with the Indians.

The Indians were happy to buy horses from the Spanish explorers. Horses helped the Indians to be better hunters and to travel from place to place.

Spanish Exploration in Western North America

Many people from Spain settled in the western and southern parts of North America. Even today, a large number of Spanish Americans live in the southwestern part of the United States. If you ever visit this part of the country, you will hear many Spanish-speaking people.

When the English settlers first reached North America, they had to build homes to live in.

The English Settlement at Jamestown, Virginia

A few years later, explorers from other nations in Europe began to sail to North America. In 1607, the first permanent English settlement was founded in the colony of Virginia. (A colony is a land that is ruled by a separate nation.) This settlement was called Jamestown.

The people from England who sailed over to start a new settlement at Jamestown had many problems. One problem started when the men began to spend their time digging for gold instead of planting food crops. As their first winter approached, many people had little or no food. They also ran into trouble with the Indians when they began to hunt for food on Indian lands.

At this time, a wise leader by the name of Captain John Smith took over the control of the tiny settlement. He forced the men to work hard in farming the land. He tried to make peace with the Indians and was able to buy corn for the settlers to eat. Without

Captain John Smith was captured by the Indians.

the help of this brave man, many people in Jamestown would have died that first winter.

Captain Smith was once held as a prisoner by a powerful Indian chief named Powhatan. The chief had decided to have John Smith killed, but his young daughter, Pocahontas, begged for the chief to spare his life. The Indian chief listened to his daughter and set Captain Smith free. Pocahontas came to Jamestown a short time later. She liked being with the people of Jamestown and fell in love with an Englishman named John Rolfe.

Pocahontas was married to this man and also came to faith in the Lord Jesus Christ. Sadly, this fine Indian woman did not live very long after her marriage. She took a trip to England with her husband and died a short time later from sickness. The people of England were sad when Pocahontas died. They used to call her "Lady Rebecca."

Captain John Smith tried to live at peace
with the Indians.

The Pilgrim Settlement in New England

In 1620, a new group of English settlers came to
the land of Massachusetts. These Englishmen were
known as the "Pilgrims," and they sailed over the
ocean on a ship called the *Mayflower*. They came
to America so they could be free to worship Jesus
Christ as the Bible commanded.

These settlers were driven out of England because
they would not worship at the king's church. For
these people, the freedom to worship and serve God
as the Bible required was more wonderful than gold
or jewels. They were willing to risk danger and even
death for the blessings of religious liberty.

When the Pilgrims landed in America, they named their settlement Plymouth. Before they left their ship, the Pilgrims wrote down a simple plan for their civil government. This plan, called "The Mayflower Compact," said that the purpose of their colony would be for "the glory of God and the advancement of the Christian faith." These wise settlers made a promise to honor Jesus Christ as the one and only

Indian warriors talk about when they should fight the English settlers.

The winter in Plymouth was very hard
for the Pilgrims.

King. The rules that were followed by the Pilgrims came from the Bible, God's Holy Word.

Like the people of Jamestown, the Pilgrims of Plymouth had a very hard time during their first winter

The first homes in Plymouth were very small and simple.

in America. Sickness, poor food, and cold weather caused many of the Pilgrims to die during the long, cold winter of 1620.

Still, these faithful Christians trusted in the Lord to help them build a beautiful colony in His good time. When springtime came, the Pilgrims went to work planting crops and building houses. A few months later, God blessed these settlers with lots of good food at harvest time. In 1621,

A friendly Indian named Squanto taught the Pilgrims how to plant corn.

Governor Bradford of Plymouth Colony ordered a day for giving thanks to God. Church services were held to thank God for His mercy in granting food and shelter. The time of worship was followed by a great big dinner.

The Pilgrims invited the Indians who lived nearby to join in their thanksgiving feast. The Indians sat quietly as the people of Plymouth prayed and sang songs of praise to God. The Indian Chief Massasoit brought a few deer to the feast and some pumpkins to eat. God in His mercy made it possible for the Indians and settlers to live at peace with one another.

The Pilgrims gathered together for a special time of thanksgiving to God.

Today, the people of the United States still celebrate "Thanksgiving Day" like the Pilgrims did over 300 years ago. Many Americans like to give thanks to God for His blessings and feast on turkey and pumpkins! Thanksgiving Day is celebrated each year on the fourth Thursday in November.

The Puritans

The Pilgrims would soon be joined by another group of Bible-believing Christians from England known as the "Puritans." This group was led by John Winthrop, who was elected governor of the Massachusetts Bay Colony. This great and kind leader helped the people organize many fine cities, schools, and churches. The famous town of Boston was founded by the Puritans, along with such colleges as Harvard and Yale.

Governor John Winthrop was a wonderful Christian who truly understood that the job of civil government was to humbly serve God and human beings. Governor Winthrop once said: "We must defend, strengthen, and comfort each other. We must love one another. We must bear one another's burdens.

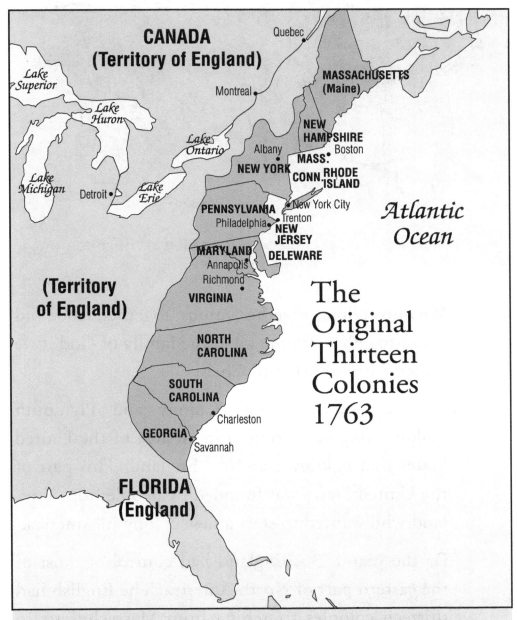

The English had set up thirteen colonies along the eastern part of North America.

Brave explorers from England often sailed at the orders of the King or Queen.

We must rejoice together, mourn together, labor and suffer together. We are all in the family of God if we all serve one another in Christ."

The Massachusetts Bay Colony and Plymouth Colony were both located in an area of the United States that is known as New England. This part of the United States was founded by people from England who wanted to start a new colony in America.

By the year 1735, England had control of most of the eastern part of North America. The English had thirteen colonies stretching from Massachusetts in the north to Georgia in the south.

Exercises

1. Ask your teacher to help you memorize the names of the thirteen English colonies. Remember that Maine was part of Massachusetts at that time.

2. Draw a picture of an old-fashioned ship sailing on the ocean.

Chapter 3 Review

12-11-15

orally

Fill in the blanks with the correct answers.

1. The term "B.C." means _Before_ _Christ_.

2. The term "A.D." stands for the words _anno_ _domino_.

3. If you were born in the year A.D. 2005, that means you were born _2,005_ years after _Christ_ was born.

4. The first explorers to sail from Europe to North America were called the _Viking_ _Norsemen (Northmen)_.

5. In 1492, another explorer from Europe named _Christopher Columbus_ rediscovered the Americas.

6. The first Spanish city in North America was called
   _____ St. Augustine _____ in 1565

7. A _____ Colony _____ is a land that is ruled by a separate nation.

8. The first permanent English settlement in North America was called _____ Jamestown _____.

9. The English people called _____ Pocahontas _____ by the name of "Lady Rebecca."

10. The Pilgrims sailed to the New World of North America on a ship called the _____ Mayflower _____.

11. The kind and loving leader of the Puritans was Governor _____ John Winthrop _____.

12. On _____ Thanksgiving _____ Day, our nation remembers the Lord for His goodness and loving care.

13. By the year 1735, England had _____ 13 _____ colonies stretching along the east coast of North America.

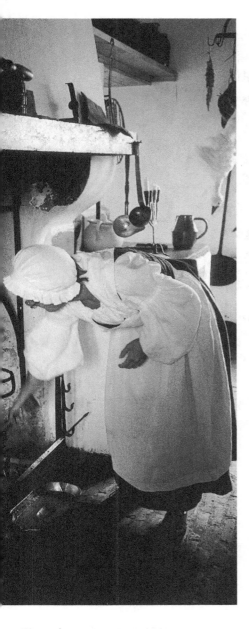

Fireplaces were very important in early America. They provided light and heat for each home and a place to cook food.

4 Others Come to America

The Lord brings the counsel of the nations to nothing; He makes the plans of the peoples of no effect. The counsel of the Lord stands forever, the plans of His heart to all generations. Blessed is the nation whose God is the Lord....
—Psalm 33:10–12a

The little ship *Half Moon* sailed across the Atlantic Ocean to America. The flag of Holland, a small nation in Europe, waved from the top of the ship. On its deck stood the captain, Henry Hudson.

Dutch Settlers in New Amsterdam and New Jersey

The *Half Moon* came to North America and sailed into a deep, wide bay. Into this bay of water flowed a beautiful river. Hudson sailed his ship up the river between high, rocky cliffs, so he named it the River of the Mountains. After he died, it was renamed the Hudson River in his honor.

Explorers from Holland set up small cities in North America so that they could trade with the Indians. The people from Holland, also called the Netherlands, are known as the Dutch people.

The Dutch merchants had many ships. They thought the area around the river would be a good place to trade with the Indians. A short time later, Dutch traders sailed from their homes in Holland and came to the Hudson River. There they met with

Indians and showed them things they could trade. The Indians liked the wonderful kettles, red blankets, knives, and hatchets that they saw. The merchants from Holland traded their things for hundreds of soft beaver and mink skins.

During one trip, the Dutch found a long, narrow island at the mouth of the Hudson River. Peter Minuit, the Dutch leader, paid the Indians a few blankets and knives for the island. The native Americans took the items and gave Minuit the island.

The Dutch named their new island Manhattan. For many years, the main city on the island was called New Amsterdam. Later on, however, the island was taken over by the nation of England and renamed New York City. This city is still called New York today, and it is the biggest city in the United States.

The French Explore the Great Lakes

The last powerful country in Europe to explore and make claims in North America was France. The king of France sent a daring sailor named Samuel de Champlain to start a French colony in North America.

Champlain's ships sailed up the great St. Lawrence River. On the north bank of this waterway he built a stone fort. A short time later, log houses were also built near the fort. Champlain named this new town Quebec. The town of Quebec is now a large city in the nation of Canada. In fact, many French explorers

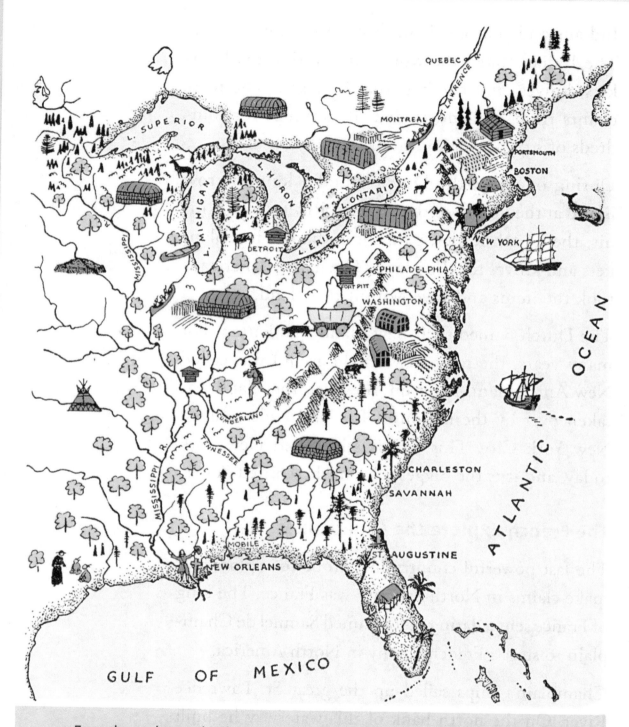

French explorers built cities in Canada around the Great Lakes.

set up cities and trading posts in Canada and in the area around the Great Lakes. One of the Great Lakes, Lake Huron, was found by Champlain himself.

The French traders who came to live near the St. Lawrence River often traded with the Indians who lived in this area. Samuel de Champlain made friends with these Indians. He sometimes took canoe trips with them. During one trip, he found a large lake and named it Lake Champlain. This brave explorer came to be called "The father of New France." New France was the name given to the area of Canada that was under the control of France.

See if you can find the Great Lakes on the map on the previous page: Lake **H**uron, Lake **O**ntario, Lake **M**ichigan, Lake **E**rie, and Lake **S**uperior. The first letter in each name of the five Great Lakes spells the word **HOMES**. If you remember this fact, it will help you to name the Great Lakes.

New Settlers

By the middle of the 1600s, North America began to get hundreds of new settlers from Europe each year. At first there were only the first Americans, or Indians, in North America. As time went by, however, more people from faraway nations wanted to come to the new world of America. Why did so many people want to move to North America? The pictures on the next page will help us to understand why people moved to North America.

Some came for the freedom to serve God and worship Him.

Some came to find good land for homes and farms.

Some came to start a new trade or business.

Some came to find gold or riches.

As we have already seen, most of the new settlers in America came from the countries of Spain, England, Holland, and France. However, most of the eastern part of North America was under the control of England.

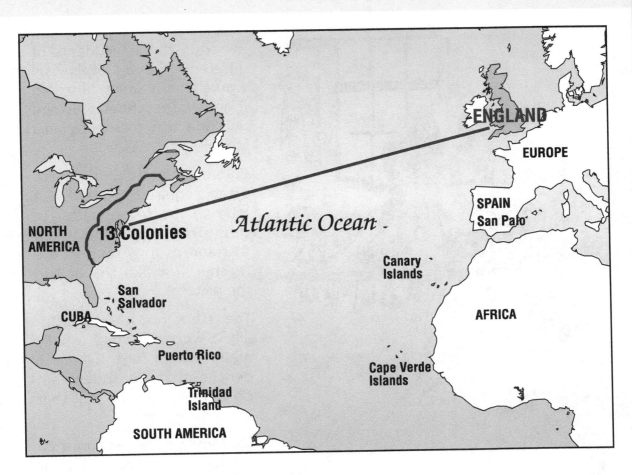

The Thirteen English Colonies

Starting in the early 1600s, the nation of England began to set up colonies like Jamestown and Plymouth along the eastern part of North America. A colony is a land that is controlled by a faraway nation. A person who lived in the American colonies when they were under English rule was called a colonist. As you can see from the map above, England was far away from her colonies.

Over a long period of time, the thirteen colonies became united into a new nation called the United States. We will learn about how the thirteen colonies became the United States and about life in colonial times.

In most schools, students of different grade levels still worked in the same classroom together. The school often had only one main teacher called a schoolmaster.

Colonial school children were often required to read out loud to the schoolmaster in class. They would be asked to stand as they read to the teacher, just like the boy in the picture.

The schoolhouse was actually a wooden cabin, usually made out of logs. Even the benches that the students sat on were made from logs that were cut in half.

Students would be punished if they did not respect their schoolmaster or do their best on their homework.

The Children of Colonial Times

Do you think that there were boys and girls among the groups of people who came to early America to make their homes? Of course there were. There were boys and girls on the *Mayflower* and on other ships that entered the colonies in New England, Virginia, Pennsylvania, and the South.

What do you think they thought when they first saw the wild and strange land of America? Do you think the Indians made them fearful? These are interesting questions to think about!

School children would often carry their reading lessons on the front of small wooden boards called "horn books." When a student was ready for the next lesson, the teacher would glue a new sheet of paper onto his horn book. These funny-looking books helped to save paper.

The parents of the colonial children were much like your parents. As soon as they had built their houses, they began to think about how to teach their children. In the homes of the Puritans and Pilgrims, there was a special desire to teach children how to read. This was due to the fact that children from these homes needed to begin to read the Bible at a young age so they could grow in wisdom.

Although most of the children in colonial times were educated at home, some church and community schools were also started. These schools often

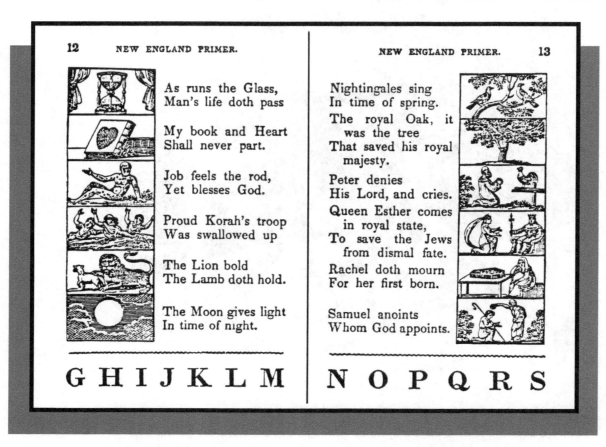

Picture of an alphabet page from the *New England Primer*

met in a log cabin with one large room. Most people call this type of school a one-room schoolhouse.

Students who lived during the colonial days had few books. They seldom had enough paper to write on, and they had to make their own pens! How did they make their own pens, you may ask? A student would take a sharp knife and cut at the end of a stick or goose feather until it had a sharp point. Then he would dip the end of the stick or feather into a small bowl of ink and begin to write.

With your teacher's help, why don't you try to find a sharp stick or feather and dip it in some ink? You can pretend that you are writing just like colonial children wrote many years ago. Be sure to have your teacher help you sharpen your "pen" so you do not get hurt with a sharp knife.

The only two books that colonial students usually had to read were the Bible and the *New England Primer*. The Primer was used for several years by colonial students. It contained reading lessons, poems, prayers, and Bible study drills. A sample page from this Primer book, showing the alphabet, is pictured on page 62.

The Most Important Day in the Week

A colonial mother worshipped God with her daughters while she sat next to her foot warmer.

Another important part of living in colonial times was keeping the Sabbath Day holy. Settlers like the Pilgrims and Puritans believed that it was their duty to rest and worship God on Sunday, the Christian Sabbath. Therefore, everyone in the colonies who loved God would gather together at their local church to worship their Maker.

Boys and girls would often help their parents on Saturday afternoon with work projects so they could rest from their work on Sunday. Large meals were also made on Saturday so that no one would have to cook on the Lord's Day. Even the farm animals were given a chance to rest on Sunday!

The church services were often two or three hours long. The preacher would pray to God and teach the people about God's Word. Boys and girls were expected to sing and pray with all their hearts and be well-behaved during the service. Most church buildings in colonial days were not heated. People brought tiny metal stoves with them filled with coals

New England still has many old buildings. A covered bridge goes over the river, and a meeting house is on the right.

from the fireplace. These stoves were put on the floor next to the family to help keep their feet warm.

Even today, many God-fearing Americans rest each Sunday and worship God at their local church building. In some parts of the country, this is why many stores are closed on Sunday and why government activities slow down as well.

How Colonial Children Played

Boys and girls of colonial times had more work to do around their home than you have. This is because they had to do many things by hand that are now done by machines or electric tools. However, these same young people played as hard as they worked.

Children in colonial days spent more time playing with each other compared to children today. After all, these children did not spend any time watching television, going to movies, or playing video games.

Perhaps it will surprise you to learn that colonial boys and girls knew more little games than you do, and they played them more often. Most of the games were the ones their grandfathers and grandmothers had played when they were children in England or Holland or some other old homeland across the sea.

Little girls, of course, had dolls. Some of these were wooden dolls that had been cut out of a piece of soft pine. Some of the little girls cut up old cloth sacks to make clothes for their dolls. Hundreds and hundreds of dolls made in Holland crossed the ocean in ships and at last found themselves in the arms of little colonial girls.

The children of early America liked to roll hoops and to spin tops. Most of the hoops and tops were homemade. The boys in those times, like many boys today, longed to own a good, sharp knife. Boys who had knives could often cut out good toys. They made willow whistles, pop-guns, windmills, and bows and arrows.

The girls, especially, knew many singing games. Here are three they liked:

"Ring around a Rosy"

"The Needle's Eye"

"London Bridge is Falling Down"

How many of these do you know? Did you ever play them and sing the words?

Other games that small boys and girls played together were hopscotch, blind man, and tag. Cat's cradle was a quiet little game for two, and was best suited to be played indoors on a winter evening.

Just as boys often do today, the boys of long ago flew kites on the first windy spring day. Their marble games were almost like yours. They played ball with a soft, homemade ball and enjoyed games such as leapfrog as much as you do.

The Dutch boys and girls who came to America brought their skates with them. The skates had wooden tops and iron blades. The winter sport of skating soon spread from the Dutch settlements to the towns and villages of their English neighbors.

Do you think that colonial boys and girls had good times, even though their games were simple and their toys often homemade?

Things to do:

1.	List the games mentioned in this story that you play today. _____ _____ _____
2.	Would it be fun to learn about the dolls of the small girls from other countries? Visit your local library to find books that will tell about the dolls from other lands.
3.	Did any of you boys ever make a toy out of wood? Tell your teacher about it or make one for the teacher.
4.	Ask your father and mother—or still better, your grandfathers and grandmothers—to tell you about the games they played. How many of them do you play?

A Winter Evening by the Fireplace

Shall we use this cold winter evening to make a visit to the home of a long-ago American family? Here we are, then, after a long walk between high snow banks. Let's look at the pictures of this colonial family on the next two pages.

The first thing we notice in the roomy kitchen is the big fireplace. It almost fills one end of the room. Near the roaring fire are all the children we have come to visit. See how busy they all are. Close to the fire we are given a seat on a bench, made from cut-up logs. When we bend over a little, we can watch the sparks as they go soaring up the wide chimney.

Hanging on chains in the fireplace are big kettles. Perched on their long legs at one side of the fire are smaller iron pots, and a number of "trivets," or three-legged iron stools. On these the food in the kettles is heated just before meal time. Leaning in a corner of the fireplace are some forks with very long handles. These are toasting forks. Why are the handles so very long?

Young girls learned to knit socks, and boys were taught how to make brooms.

What are the little girls in the previous picture doing? It will be hard for you to guess what the boy in the previous picture is making. He is making an "Indian broom!" With his knife he is splitting one end of a straight piece of birch wood into fine slivers. With this strange broom his mother will sweep the floor tomorrow morning.

Dad makes shoes while Mom makes thread
for clothing.

What is the mother doing in the picture above? The father seems to be making a pair of heavy shoes. The blaze in the fireplace gives them almost all the light they need. There is also a small candle hanging on the wall and a metal lantern on the floor.

The lantern can be carried all over the house. Families often burned the oil that comes from whales in their lanterns.

And now it is time for the family to go to bed. After a good visit, we start for home over the crunchy snow. Then this long-ago family gets ready for bed. First of all, father covers the fire with ashes so it will not go out. The mother puts live coals in the warming pan, hurries to the beds, and passes the pan up and down and all around between the icy-cold blankets to take away a little of the cold. Next, a great oak bar is set in place against the door, and one by one the candles are "snuffed." Now the members of the family scamper from the warm kitchen to their beds for a long night's sleep.

Activity

Orally

1-19-16

What did the early settlers use for:

1.	light?	*lanterns / a large fireplace / candles*
2.	brooms?	*birch wood*
3.	heat?	*fireplace*
4.	chairs?	*split logs*
5.	cooking?	*fireplace + pots*
6.	locks?	*oak bar*

Talking with the Fishermen

Many of the colonial boys and girls lived in towns right on the shore of the ocean. Almost every safe, deep harbor had a village near it. At times, the waters of the harbors were almost covered with boats and small ships. These were the fishing vessels, and they belonged to the fathers and older brothers of the village children. Nearly every family in such a village made its living from fishing.

"School, o-oh!" This sounds like a call to hurry to school, but it is not. It was the shout of a mackerel fisherman when he saw a "school" of mackerel. When this call sounded, the great nets were let down from the boats, spread out, and then lifted. If the fishermen were blessed, their nets would contain hundreds and hundreds of mackerel.

Hunting for whales was hard and dangerous work.

Cod, herring, and other fish were also caught with nets and hooks by the colonial fishermen. After the fish had been cleaned, they were dried and salted in sheds along the shore. After a time, the fish were taken to markets in Europe or in the West Indies.

How happy the children were when the fishing boats came back to the harbor after their long voyages on the stormy ocean! We may be quite sure they beat everyone else in the village in the race to the wharves to greet the coming boats. There they met fathers and brothers home from the sea, looked at the cargoes of fish, and watched the fishermen as they wound their nets.

Back to some of the little fishing towns came the whalers. The men who went away on voyages to capture whales were called whalers, of course. The stout ships they went in were called whalers, too. Every boy in the village felt proud if he could say that his father or brother was a whaler.

In very early times, the great whales came close to the shore where the settlers lived. Sometimes they were even washed up on the shore by the waves and could not get back. But in later colonial days, hunting whales was likely to take the whalers on voyages covering thousands of miles.

Mystic Seaport in Connecticut has a display of an old ship.

When they came home with their ships filled with barrels of whale oil, they had wonderful stories to tell about going close up to the whales in small boats and driving their spears deep into the sides of the monsters. Often a wounded whale would tow a boat miles and miles through the sea before it gave up. Almost every boy hoped that he would one day be brave enough to become a whaler.

Work That Was Play

Most of the early settlers in colonial America were poor people who had to work hard for a living. There were many tasks for the children and their fathers and mothers. On the farms there were chickens, pigs, and calves to feed and weeds to pull out of the patches of corn and potatoes. When the wheat and oats were cut in the fields, one of the tasks of the older boys was to bind the grain into bundles.

Colonial boys gathered firewood for the fireplace at home.

In most American homes, children were expected to carry in wood for the fireplaces and to bring in water from the wells. Even small girls in most colonial homes helped clean the clothes. They stirred the big kettle when soap was being made, helped dip candles, and aided their mothers in ways girls help their mothers today.

It does not seem likely that the boys and girls of long ago liked their steady round of tasks any better than you do. But then, they did other helpful things that must have been fun for them.

In the summertime wild berries were to be gathered. Among the stumps in the fields wild strawberries could be found. In the brushy places the children found raspberries, and sometimes in the swamps they gathered the red cranberries. How pleased the mothers must have been to have the children come home from their berry picking with their wooden pails filled with wild berries!

Cool October evenings brought the corn huskings. The young people gathered on the floor of a barn and there husked the yellow ears of corn. This was useful work, too, and the boys and girls of long ago made a game of it.

On many of the small northern farms stood fine groves of maple trees. The farmers did not cut down

Most mothers in colonial days made clothes for the entire family.

these trees, for the maple sap could be gathered in the early spring and boiled until it became maple syrup or maple sugar. The children were always on hand when the owner of the grove "sugared off," or finished the boiling of the sap. From the bottom of the kettle came warm, syrupy maple sugar for all. Then there was a fun time as the children played among the big trees and circled about the roaring fire.

This peaceful old town in New England is a beautiful sight.

Nice!

1-27-16

Chapter 4 Review

Fill in the blanks with the correct answers.

1. Henry __Hudson__ sailed from Holland to North America on a ship called the *Half Moon*.

2. The Dutch city of New Amsterdam was renamed __New York__ after it was taken over by the English.

3. Samuel de Champlain was sent by the King of __France__ to set up a colony in North America.

4. The Pilgrims and Puritans wanted their children to be able to read at a young age so they could understand the __Bible__.

5. The Bible and __New England Primer__ were the two main books used by school students in colonial days.

6. __Sunday__ was the most important day of the week to colonial Americans who loved God.

7. Colonial families cooked their meals in large pots over the __Fire__.

8. Many colonial children lived in towns very near the Atlantic __Ocean__.

5 The War for Freedom

Therefore if the Son makes you free, you shall be free indeed.—John 8:36

Life in colonial America was hard, but the Lord blessed the work of the American people. Slowly but surely, the small, dirt-floored cabins of the settlers were replaced by bigger and nicer homes. Good roads were built from one busy town to another, and farmers used better tools to grow more food.

Still, many of the colonial people were not happy with the way their government was working. The king of England, King George III, was a foolish leader of the colonies. He said that the colonies had to follow his unfair rules and pay him money in taxes. One of the king's rules said that the colonists had to sell their food and man-made goods to business people in England who were the king's friends. This made the colonists angry, for they wanted the freedom to sell their things to whoever they felt was willing to give them a fair price. The king also began to put people that he hated in prison without giving them a fair trial.

The colonists wanted to be free from the king of England and his unjust laws. These Americans wanted a country that had no other king but Jesus.

It soon became clear that King George thought that the colonists were his slaves. The leaders in America tried to talk with the king about their problems, but he would not listen. Instead, he tried even harder to force the colonies to submit to his plans. When the colonial leaders saw that the king was sending over large groups of soldiers who were trying to take away the people's guns, they knew they had to fight.

One of the greatest colonial leaders, Patrick Henry, told the Americans that if they wanted to be free, they would have to go to war. In 1775, shortly before the War for American Independence began, Henry made a great speech. He said, "Is life so dear, or peace so sweet as to be purchased at the price of chains and slavery? Forbid it, Almighty God! I know not what course others may take; but as for me, give me liberty or give me death!"

The Declaration of Independence

In the year 1775, American colonists began to fight for their freedom from English rule. The colonial leaders, led by Thomas Jefferson, wrote a paper to King George called the Declaration of Independence. This paper said that

Benjamin Franklin was a famous American patriot who helped to start the United States. He worked as a printer and ran his own newspaper in Philadelphia. This picture shows Franklin working in his print shop.

the American colonies were no longer under English rule. It said that the colonies were now united into a new nation called the United States of America. The Declaration was signed on July 4, 1776. This day is now celebrated as our country's birthday.

The king of England read this paper and decided to continue fighting with the American colonists to force them to stay under his control. God was good to the Americans and they fought bravely. They were willing to die for their freedom. As the war began, the Lord also gave the people of America the desire to start their own nation and set up a new system of law and government.

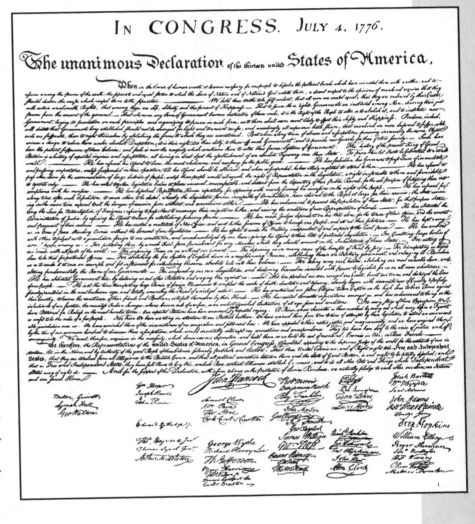

A declaration is an important message.

Independence means you are free to live as God requires.

The Declaration of Independence says that God alone is the One who gives people their rights. The colonists believed that the Lord gives all people three basic rights:

1.	The right to life
2.	The right to liberty
	(to be free from rules made by evil men)
3.	The right to seek happiness
	(to own things like land, houses, and guns)

The War for Independence

The leader of the American armies was a fine Christian man who often prayed to God. His name was General George Washington. God always protected this good leader from harm. The enemy's bullets came close to him many times, but the Lord kept him safe.

The British army was big and had powerful guns. The colonial army was small and did not always have the best cannons or rifles. The country of

The minutemen were common farmers and businessmen who were ready and willing to fight for American freedoms. The name "minuteman" came from the idea that these citizen soldiers could be ready to fight anywhere in just a minute.

The Battle of Lexington was only one of many battles in the great War for American Independence.

France, however, sent soldiers and ships to help the colonial army fight the British. George Washington's army suffered in many ways, but he was always there to encourage his troops. After many years of fighting, the king's army gave up and went back to England. God had given victory to the American colonies in the great War for Independence. A peace treaty was signed in 1783 that brought the fighting to an end.

Now the colonies could be joined together into a group of united states. The big pieces of land that made up each of the thirteen colonies would now be called states.

George Washington was put in charge of the colonial army. After the War for American Independence, Washington was chosen to be the first President of the United States.

The Flag and the Constitution

Our new country was made up of thirteen independent states. This new country, therefore, needed a new flag. The flag pictured here is what the first flag of the United States looked like.

Many people believe that the first flag was made by a lady named Betsy Ross.

■ Activities

1.	Draw a picture of the first American flag.
2.	Read a short book on the life of George Washington.
3.	In a sentence, explain why the first flag of the United States had only thirteen stars.

The New Government

The government of the United States of America would be a new and different kind of government. For the first time in history, government leaders would truly let people be free. The rules of our new government were written down on four large pieces of paper and are called the Constitution of the United States. This important paper said that the government's power to control the American people would be very small. The government would need to get permission from the people before it could take control of or tax any American citizen. Government leaders would not be given kingly powers to rule over the people.

The leaders of early America believed that each person was given rights by Almighty God. These leaders understood that the job of government was to protect the God-given rights of the people.

On July 4, 1776, a big bell rang in the city of Philadelphia to announce the signing of the Declaration of Independence. We now call this bell the Liberty Bell, because it was the first to ring in American freedom. Many years after the American War for Independence, this famous bell was cracked. The Liberty Bell is an important symbol of the American nation.

The Constitution is the most important law of the land, next to the laws contained in the Holy Bible. The important laws in our Constitution protect us from evil and selfish leaders who may wish to make us slaves. One wonderful part of the Constitution says that the American people have the right to choose their own leaders. When the people of America choose their leaders, it is called voting in an election.

For example, the highest leader in the United States is called our President. He is chosen by the American people but can only serve as President for four years. Then he must go to the people again to see if they want him to stay President. If the people vote in favor of the President, he can stay. If they vote against him, however, he will lose all of his power to serve the people.

In many other nations, the people are not free to vote. These people are told by the government who will be their next king. People in these nations are like servants to the king. Leaders in the United States, however, are servants to the people. Our Constitution is based upon an understanding that sinful men cannot be trusted with too much power. The Constitution, therefore, limits the power of each person who is given the right to serve the people of the United States. Under the Constitution, our government has worked well.

The Constitution also has an important section called the Bill of Rights. This section lists some of the most important rights or freedoms that are promised to every citizen. In 1791, the Bill of Rights was added to our great Constitution. Study the original Bill of Rights as listed below.

The Bill of Rights

1.	The right to worship and serve God freely, the right of free speech and press, the right to gather together in a peaceful way to ask the government to correct a problem
2.	The right to own and carry guns and weapons

3.	The right to keep government soldiers out of our homes
4.	The right to own private property and to keep it secure from unreasonable searches and seizures
5.	The right to be considered innocent of a crime until you are proven guilty by a proper court
6.	The right to a fair and speedy trial
7.	The right to a trial by jury
8.	The right to be kept free from unreasonable bail or punishment
9.	The rights or powers of government are limited by the people, but the people's rights are not limited to those written in the Constitution
10.	The powers of the federal government are limited by the Constitution, with the remaining powers going to the states or to the people

The War of 1812

In the year 1812, a new war broke out again between the United States and England. This war, however, was not as large or long-lasting as the War for American Independence. By early 1815, the British army had fought its last battle with the United States. Once again God gave victory to the United States in this second war with England. Never again would these two countries fight a war against each other.

Patriotic Song:
"The Star Spangled Banner"

Words by Francis Scott Key

"The Star Spangled Banner" is our nation's theme song. We call it our national anthem because it tells the world about our country.

Francis Scott Key was a young lawyer when he wrote our nation's song in September 1814. He wrote down this song while he was watching the battle between the Americans and the British in Baltimore, Maryland. England was at war with our country again, and several British ships were trying to take over a fort that guarded the people of Baltimore. As the cannons roared and the bombs exploded, Mr. Key wondered if the American flag would still be flying over Baltimore after the battle was done. By God's grace, the British ships and cannonballs were not able to win this battle.

When Francis Scott Key saw that his country's flag was still flying free after the battle, he was filled with joy. He went on to finish his song, and his friends enjoyed it so much that they began to print copies for others in Baltimore. Soon "The Star Spangled Banner" was being printed and sung all over the United States. Ask your teacher to help you sing the two verses from this song that are given below.

The Star Spangled Banner

O say can you see, by the dawn's early light,
What so proudly we hailed at the twilight's last gleaming?
Whose broad stripes and bright stars,
through the perilous fight,
O'er the ramparts we watched were so gallantly streaming!
And the rocket's red glare, the bombs bursting in air,
Gave proof through the night that our flag was still there:

O say, does that star-spangled banner yet wave
O'er the land of the free and the home of the brave?

O thus be it ever, when freemen shall stand
Between their loved homes and the war's desolation!
Blest with victory and peace, may the heaven-rescued land
Praise the Power that hath made and preserved us a nation.
Then conquer we must, when our cause it is just,
And this be our motto: "In God is our trust,"
And the star-spangled banner in triumph shall wave
O'er the land of the free and the home of the brave!

A team of skilled artists carved a monument to four American Presidents in Mt. Rushmore. This famous American monument is in the state of South Dakota.

Chapter 5 Review

2-11-2016

Fill in the blanks with the correct answers.

orally

1. The American colonists were ruled by King ___George III___ of England in the year 1775.

2. When the king's soldiers tried to steal the colonists' ___weapons___ they knew they had to fight.

3. The great colonial leader, ___Patrick Henry___, told the Americans that if they wanted to be free they would have to go to war.

4. The colonial leaders wrote a paper to King George called the ___Declaration of Independence___. This paper said that the colonies were now united into a new nation called the United States of America.

5. ___God___ alone is the One who gives people their rights.

6. The leader of the American armies was a fine Christian named General ___Washington___.

7. "The Star Spangled Banner" was written by ___Francis Scott Key___.

8. The ___Constitution___ is the most important law of the land in the United States.

9. The act of choosing new leaders in the U.S. is done through ___voting___.

6 Pioneers Fill America

Be fruitful and multiply; fill the earth and subdue it....—Genesis 1:28b

As more people came to America, the once small cities of early America began to grow very big. Cities like New York, Philadelphia, and Boston began to seem crowded. People began to think about moving their families into the huge western part of North America.

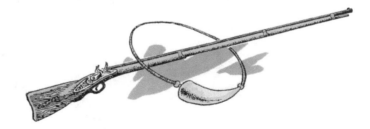

Thousands of people living in the eastern part of the United States moved west in covered wagons during the 1800s. Families going west often traveled together in large groups called wagon trains.

The great western lands had beautiful open areas for farming, but they also had Indians. Only the bravest of pioneers were willing to be among the first to load up a wagon and head out for wilderness lands. A pioneer is someone who is willing be the first person to go into a new land so others can follow. The story of the American pioneer is really a story of how our nation grew across the continent of North America.

Daniel Boone was a great hunter and explorer. He helped to make a path in the wilderness for others to follow.

Daniel Boone Explores

The lands or territories of Kentucky and Tennessee were among the first to be explored by early pioneers. In the late 1770s, a brave pioneer named Daniel Boone led thirty men to clear a path through the thick woods of Kentucky. They cut down many trees so people could ride out west in their covered wagons. The trail they made in the wilderness was called the Wilderness Road. As the years passed, thousands of pioneer families used this road to travel west.

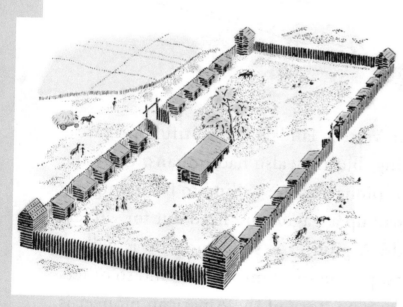

The first fort built in the Kentucky wilderness to help pioneers who were moving west was called Boonesborough.

By the early 1800s, thousands of families were heading to new lands in the West. Soon families were moving into parts of the Ohio territory and into other lands held by the Indians. Some pioneers treated the Indians fairly and paid for the land they took. Some pioneers, however, did not pay for the land they took and lied to the Indians or killed them.

The Wilderness Road was simply a path cut in the woods for pioneers to follow.

The United States government tried to work out land issues with the Indians but was often unable to stop settlers who wanted to steal from or hurt native Americans. Slowly, the Indians were forced to move farther and farther west. A few Indian tribes tried to fight a war with the American government, but they were unable to win because they had few guns and no cannon.

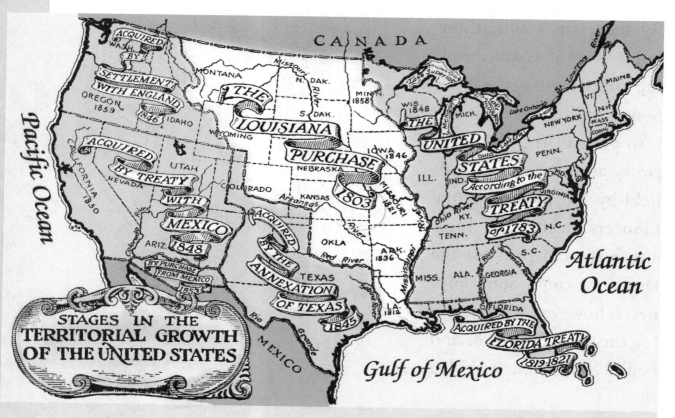

The Louisiana Purchase added a large area of land to the United States.

Westward Ho!

At this same time, the ruler of France sold the United States government a large piece of land in the central part of North America. This land deal was called "The Louisiana Purchase," and it made our country almost twice as big. Study the map above to see how much bigger the United States became after it obtained the Louisiana territory.

The move of people into the western lands was at a slow rate until the American people built the first railroad across the continent from east to west. This railroad was completed in 1869, making it possible

A wagon trail called the National Pike was used by thousands of people to travel into the western wilderness.

for settlers to travel from the State of New York to California in one week instead of three months. This opened up the West to almost anyone who wanted to go. We must, however, not forget the brave pioneers who first opened the West for others to follow.

The railroad helped pioneers to travel west more quickly.

The growth of railroads also helped people in the West who raised huge herds of cattle. Before the railroads were built, it was very hard for ranchers to get their cattle to market. Once the railroads were in place, however, the cattle ranchers could hire cowboys to take their herds of cattle to the closest town that had a railroad. The cattle would be sold at the markets in town and then shipped by train to meat packing centers all over the United States. This helped the business of raising and selling cattle to grow very fast.

The Cowboy

Many wonderful songs and movies have been made about the exciting adventures of cowboys who lived in the "Wild West." When cattlemen and cowboys were not riding the open fields on a cattle drive, they were often faced with many hardships. It was not easy to be a cowboy in the 1800s.

The American cowboy helped to move cattle across the country to be sold at market. Moving herds of cattle was often called a "cattle drive."

Sometimes the cowboys would have to fight with Indians who did not want them to take cattle across their lands. Still, many men dearly loved the freedom and adventure of riding their horses across the land. They enjoyed sleeping under the stars.

The buffalo or bison once roamed the great western lands in large herds.

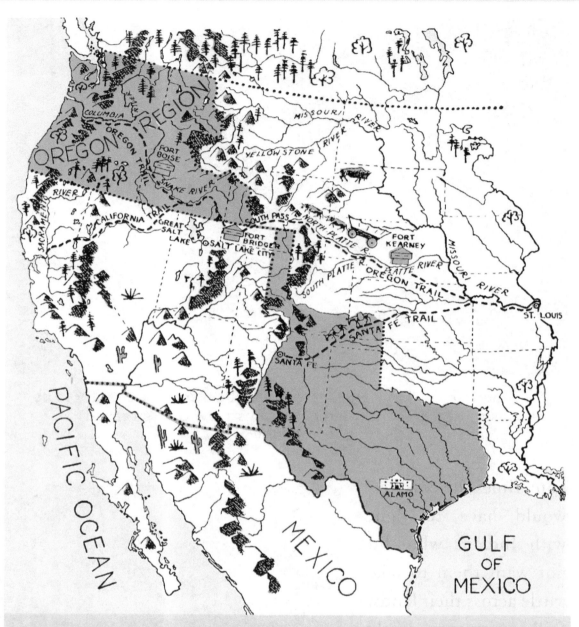

Pioneers moving west often traveled on special trails. The most popular trails were the Oregon Trail, the Santa Fe Trail, and the California Trail.

The California Gold Rush

Railroads were not the only reason why the western part of the United States began to be settled. In the year 1848, a group of miners discovered gold as they were digging in the hills of California. Very soon, thousands of Americans began to travel to California to find gold.

Not everyone who took part in the so-called "gold rush" found riches. However, many of the people who went to California found a beautiful place to live. By 1850, the California territory was so settled by pioneers that it was allowed to become the thirty-first state in the Union.

Other territories were added to our country in the 1800s. Florida was bought from Spain in the year 1819. The Oregon Territory was acquired from England in 1846. In 1845 Texas was added to the United States; and, in 1848, the great Southwest territory was added.

Families often moved west in covered wagons during the 1800s. What things would you bring with you if you were going west? Remember, everything you want to bring has to fit in your wagon!

Growth of Railroads

Railroads were built all over the United States to help our nation grow. Can you see how many new railroads were added throughout the U.S. since 1870?

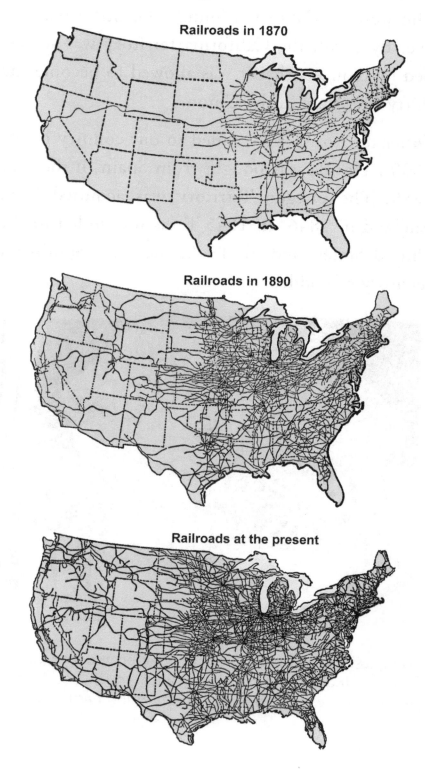

Railroads in 1870

Railroads in 1890

Railroads at the present

Patriotic Song:
"My Country 'Tis of Thee"

Words by Samuel Francis Smith

The song "My Country 'Tis of Thee" is not written about war or the brave acts of men. Rather, it is a hymn that tells people how much we love our nation, our liberty, and our Great God and King, Jesus Christ.

The author of this hymn wrote "My Country 'Tis of Thee" in 1832 while he was studying to be a Christian minister. Mr. Smith wrote this song in just a few minutes. He never thought that it would someday be sung by people all across the United States. Ask your teacher to help you sing this beautiful American hymn.

My country 'tis of thee,
Sweet land of liberty,
    Of thee I sing;
Land where my fathers died,
Land of the pilgrims' pride
From every mountainside
    Let freedom ring.

My native country, thee,
Land of the noble free,
    Thy name I love;
I love thy rocks and rills,
Thy woods and templed hills;
My heart with rapture thrills
    Like that above.

Let music swell the breeze,
And ring from all the trees
    Sweet freedom's song;
Let mortal tongues awake,
Let all that breathe partake,
Let rocks their silence break—
    The sound prolong.

Our fathers' God, to Thee,
Author of liberty,
    To Thee we sing;
Long may our land be bright
With freedom's holy light;
Protect us by Thy might,
    Great God, our King.

Slaves worked on some southern farms growing tobacco or picking cotton. Southern farmers with large fields foolishly refused to give their slaves freedom.

The War Between the North and the South

One problem that caused the American people to think less about moving west was a war that broke out between the states. In 1860, after the election of Abraham Lincoln as our new President, the states in the southern part of the country decided to leave the Union. They set up a new nation called the Confederate States of America.

The people in the South felt that the government of the United States was growing too big and powerful. The Southern states also believed that each state should have the power to control its own people.

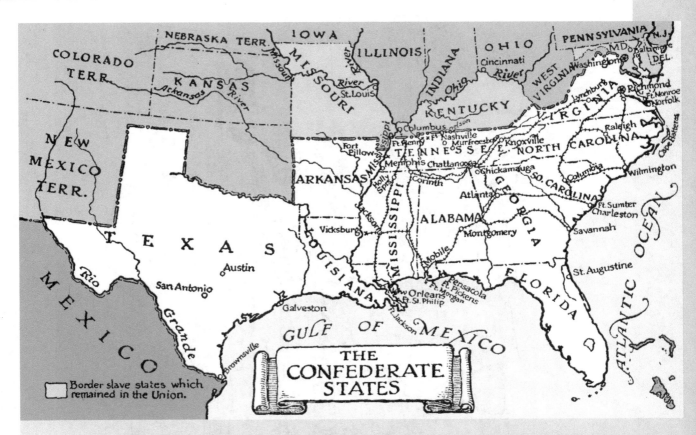

The Confederate States of America tried to leave the United States.

Leaders in the South benefited from the power that the Constitution gave them to own slaves. Many Southern people, therefore, did not want to set their slaves free because they needed them to work as cooks and farmhands. For this and other reasons, they decided to leave the United States in an effort to keep their rights as free states.

President Lincoln and other Northern leaders told the South that it could not leave the Union.

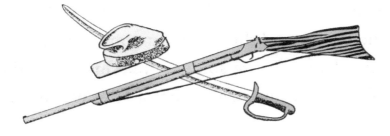

President Abraham Lincoln and his generals
talked about the best way to fight against the
Southern states.

Later on, Mr. Lincoln also told the Southern leaders that they would have to set their slaves free. A long and bloody war was fought, and thousands of Americans died.

General "Stonewall" Jackson and General Robert E. Lee helped to lead the Southern army in its fight for independence. These soldiers, like many Southern people, did not own slaves. Before the War Between

General "Stonewall" Jackson was a brave Christian who fought for Southern independence. Like Robert E. Lee, General Jackson was respected by Americans in the North and South.

the States, Mr. Jackson taught black children at his church during Sunday school.

The Confederate states had the right to leave the Union. However, they did not have the right to support slavery. God judged the South for its stubbornness in refusing to turn away from slavery.

The War Between the States caused much suffering and sadness in our beloved country.

The Northern army, under the command of General Ulysses S. Grant, was much larger than the Southern army. In the end, the North was able to force the South to rejoin the Union, and the slaves were set free. By God's grace, the American people were able to put our nation back together.

Patriotic Song: "Dixie"

Words and music by
Daniel Decatur Emmett

Daniel Emmett lived in the 1800s and worked as a stage actor and songwriter. One cold winter night in the year 1858, Mr. Emmett was walking along the streets of New York City. Suddenly, he began to think of the warmer weather in the southern part of America and said, "I wish I was in Dixie." These words gave him the idea he needed for a new song.

He began to add words and write music for his new song "Dixie." The song was well liked by the people who heard him sing it on stage. The southern people liked it even more than the people who lived in the northern part of the country. During the War Between the States, therefore, "Dixie" became the famous Confederate battle song. After the war, the song was played and sung all over the United States.

Ask your teacher to help you sing this song.

"Dixie"

I wish I was in the land of cotton,
Old times there are not forgotten;
Look away, look away, look away,
Dixie land!

In Dixie land where I was born in,
Early on one frosty mornin',
Look away, look away, look away,
Dixie land!

This world was made in just six days,
And finished up in various ways.
Look away! look away! look away!
Dixie land!

Then they made Dixie trim and nice
And Adam called it "Paradise."
Look away, look away, look away,
Dixie land!

There's buckwheat cakes and Injun batter,
Makes you fat or a little fatter;
Look away, look away, look away,
Dixie land!

Then hoe it down and scratch your gravel,
To Dixie's land I'm bound to travel;
Look away, look away, look away,
Dixie land!

(chorus)
Then I wish I was in Dixie! Hooray! Hooray!
In Dixie's land we'll take our stand, to live and die in Dixie,
Away, away, away, down south in Dixie!
Away, away, away, down south in Dixie!

3-16-16

Chapter 6 Review

Fill in the blanks with the correct answers.

orally

1. A ___pioneer___ is willing to go into a new land before other people are ready.

2. A brave explorer named ___Daniel Boone___ helped to lead pioneer families into Kentucky and Tennessee.

3. Some of the pioneer families treated the ___Indians___ unfairly.

4. The United States grew twice as big when it bought the ___Louisiana Purchase___ from the ruler of France.

5. The first American railroad running from east to west was finished in ___1869___.

6. The ___South___ decided to leave the Union and start a new nation called the Confederate States of America.

7. President ___Abraham Lincoln___'s Northern army fought a big war to keep the Southern states from leaving the United States.

8. The War Between the States helped slaves to gain their ___freedom___.

9. Mr. Daniel Emmett wrote the song "___Dixie___."

The invention of the steamboat made it possible for Americans to travel up and down rivers quickly.

7 Inventions Help America

What is man that You are mindful of him, and the son of man that You visit him? For You have made him a little lower than the angels, and You have crowned him with glory and honor. You have made him to have dominion over the works of Your hands; You have put all things under his feet, all sheep and oxen—even the beasts of the field, the birds of the air, and the fish of the sea that pass through the paths of the seas. —Psalm 8:4–8

The American people were blessed with the freedom to live their dreams. God blessed the United States with people who could think of new ways of getting things done. When someone finds a better way to make things or do things we call this an invention.

From the early 1800s to the early 1900s, life in America changed a great deal because of inventions. Let's look at just a few of the great inventions that helped America to grow.

Eli Whitney Invents the Cotton Gin

One person could clean five pounds of cotton daily.

Cotton is often used to make clothes. Eli Whitney made a machine called the cotton gin that could quickly clean out seeds from the cotton. Now clothes

The cotton gin cleaned one hundred pounds per day.

could be made faster, and they would cost less because cotton was easier to clean and prepare for use. The cotton gin helped Americans enjoy the blessing of good clothes at a good price.

Robert Fulton Invents the Steamboat

The steamboat was the first boat with an engine to make it move. Before the steamboat, big ships needed wind to move them. Now people could travel by boat anytime, even if the wind was not blowing. Steamboats helped Americans travel quickly around the United States by riding up and down rivers and lakes.

Robert Fulton built the first successful steamboat in the year 1807. The powerful steamships made it possible for Americans to move heavy things like steel and logs from place to place. As more people moved into the western part of the United States, they used

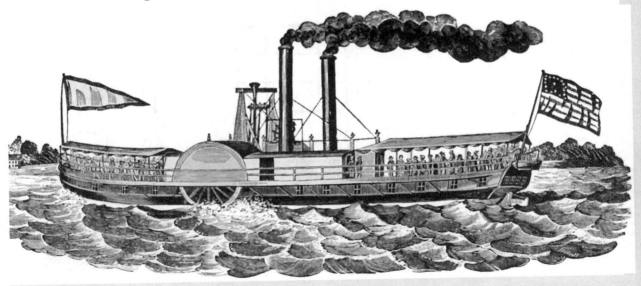

The steamships were often called "paddle boats" because they had long wooden paddles that turned under the water to make them move.

steamships to carry the things they needed to build new homes. Steamships helped people build cities and factories all across America.

Samuel Morse Invents the Telegraph

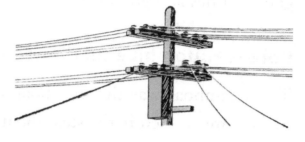

The telegraph made it possible to send messages to many faraway places through electrical wires. Now people could get a message to someone far away very fast. The first words that Samuel Morse sent over his telegraph wires were: "What hath God wrought?" This means, "Look at what new thing God has shown us!" Mr. Morse put up the first telegraph lines in the year 1844.

Professor Morse works on his new invention, the telegraph.

Alexander Graham Bell Invents the Telephone

In the late 1800s, an invention that was even more wonderful than the telegraph was created. The telephone made it possible for people to talk directly to others far away with their own voices! The older telegraph could only send messages by way of special "clicking" sounds. The telephone made it easier and faster for people to talk with each other. Have you ever talked to someone far away with the telephone? If so, write down the city, state, and country that you called with your telephone.

Early telephones were not very powerful. They would only let people talk to other people in a few areas of the United States.

City ___Carterville___

State ___Illinois___

Country ___U. S.___

Callid Nani—

Modern telephones are powerful. They will let people talk to others all over the world.

Thomas Alva Edison, the great Inventor

Thomas Edison Invents the Light Bulb

Mr. Edison was a great inventor. Perhaps his greatest invention was the electric light bulb. In 1879, Thomas Edison found out how to send electricity through a thin piece of wire, covered by glass, and cause light to shine out of it. No longer would people need to use the old oil lamps that were so dirty and dangerous. The electric light bulb helps people to read, work, or play in the daytime or at night.

Early lightbulbs looked like this.

The first popular American cars were called Model T's. They could only move slightly faster than a quick horse, but they were fun to drive!

The Automobile Was Made in America by Henry T. Ford

Ever since the days of the early Spanish explorers, people in America used horses to take them from place to place. Thanks to the efforts of Henry T. Ford in the late 1800s and early

Modern automobiles can move very fast.

1900s, he helped to put Americans on wheels! The car or automobile was much faster than the horse and would not get "tired" as quickly. Therefore, this invention made it possible for common Americans to travel long distances without stopping. Mr. Ford invented a way to make cars quickly and cheaply.

The first planes were only able to carry one or two people because their engines were weak.

Orville and Wilbur Wright Invent the Airplane

People have always wanted to fly like the birds. However, God held back the secret of flight from men until the year 1903. In that year,

Modern airplanes can carry many people and fly much faster than the first planes.

two young men from Ohio were able to build and fly the first airplane. The airplane helped to move people and things across the United States and even across the wide world. The airplane helped America to grow.

George Washington Carver, From Slave to Inventor

Wright Brothers Memorial at Kitty Hawk, North Carolina

George Washington Carver was born a slave shortly before the War Between the States. His parents died when he was young, and he lived in the home of

George Washington Carver discovered how to use plants for the good of others.

friends who were very poor. Still, God was with George Carver and gave him the strength to rise above his problems.

George worked very hard and studied hard as well. He loved to read science books, especially those that told about plants and animals. When Mr. Carver grew up, he went to college to study about the wonders of God's creation, the wonders of plants and how things grow.

Great inventors can make useful things out of simple plants like peanuts.

After college, George Carver worked as a teacher at the Tuskegee Institute and became an inventor as he unlocked the secrets of plants. He showed people how to make many kinds of useful things from plants. For example, he taught how to make hundreds of useful things from peanuts. Mr. Carver discovered how to make soap, butter, chocolate, ink, and candy—all from peanuts!

He also helped farmers by telling them which crops to grow on their farms. When American farmers listened to the wisdom of this great inventor and teacher, they grew more food and had a better life. The reason why George Washington Carver was able to discover such great things was because he loved God and people. He called the place where he labored "God's Little Workshop."

These are only a few of the inventions that were made during the 1800s and early 1900s. God used these inventions to bless the American people. Life was much better because people could grow food faster and make clothes for less money than before. Inventions also helped Americans to move from place to place more quickly and to talk with people who were far away.

Immigrants Come to America from Many Lands

The United States was starting to grow bigger and stronger as the year 1900 began a new century. God-given freedom gave people the desire to try new things and create modern inventions. During the late 1800s, millions of people from throughout the world left their homes to come to America. These new Americans were called immigrants. An immigrant is a person from another land who moves into a new country and sets up his home.

Many people from around the world move to the United States each year. They come to our nation to find the blessings of freedom.

The Statue of Liberty is located in New York City. This huge metal statue was given to our nation by the people of France. It is an important symbol of our nation.

These immigrants worked hard to build good things like churches, good roads and bridges, and railroads. They also worked in factories making things like steel, paper products, and furniture. Many immigrants also worked as farmers or raised cattle to feed hungry people. Life was not always easy for these new Americans. They had to learn how to speak the English language and save up the money

Factories are big buildings where workers make things that people need.

to buy food and homes. Still, for many, they grew
to love the United States, "The Land of the Free!"

Farms are Important to the United States

The United States has surely been blessed with lots of good farmland. This is one of the reasons why people want to live and work in the United States. American farms produce much of the food and materials that people in the United States need. The map on the following page shows you where crops and forests are often grown in the United States.

Big trucks take the food crops like corn, wheat, and citrus to factories where they can be cleaned and prepared for sale. Crops like cotton are harvested by farmers who then send

In the 1700s, a farmer could only grow enough food for his own family.

In the 1800s, better inventions helped a single farmer to grow enough food for three families.

In the 1900s, the invention of the tractor helped each farmer to grow enough food for sixteen families.

This map shows us where many crops are grown in the United States. It also shows us where most of the big forests are located. Trees provide us with the wood we need to build houses and make paper products like the book you are reading.

the cotton to special factories. The people who work in these factories make clothes from the cotton.

Lumberjacks cut down trees in forest areas and send the logs to special factories called sawmills. The factory workers cut the logs into smooth boards and send them to shops that make furniture and other wooden things.

The clothes and things that are made from wood are then sold to store owners who in turn sell these products to Americans.

In 1831, a great inventor named Cyrus McCormick made the first machine to cut and bundle wheat. This machine was called a reaper. It helped farmers harvest their wheat crops much faster than by hand. Modern reaping machines are pulled by big tractors rather than horses.

American farmers and factory workers work so hard that they are also able to produce food and household things for people outside the United States. Every year, people in other countries buy many kinds of food and products that were made in America. Thankfully, American workers have the freedom to work and make a good life for themselves as they sell the things that they make.

Before the invention of the reaper, farmers had to cut and bundle all of their crops of grain by hand.

Farmers are very important. They grow the food that we need so we can buy it at produce and grocery stores.

The American Indians

What, you may ask, happened to the first Americans? The American Indians were forced to move farther and farther west and were given poor lands on which to live. The Indians were often treated badly in the 1800s. After the year 1900, however, our nation finally started to deal fairly with the Indians. The United States government would often pay the Indians for the land they lost instead of just taking it from them. Our government leaders even helped the Indians by sending them money to build churches. These leaders also gave them thousands of Bibles so they could learn about God.

Many American Indians came to faith in Jesus Christ and had their sins taken away. Soon the Indians began to build new homes, schools, and libraries for their people. God used the hard times that the Indians went through to humble them and make them ready to hear His Word. The Lord also taught the people of the United States a lesson about how important it is to treat people honestly. When God commanded people to "love their neighbor," He was surely including people like the American Indians!

One Nation Under God

Everyone who is born in the United States is a citizen of the United States. People who were not born in the United States can still become citizens if they move here and pass a test given by the government. The United States is one great country made up of many different people from around the world. Together we are "one nation under God...."

The famous Indian leader Geronimo (1829–1909) became a Christian late in life. He joined the Indian Reformed Church. When he died, he was given a Christian burial.

Many Americans who are proud of their country fly a flag from their homes.

Patriotic Song: "America the Beautiful"

Words by Katharine Lee Bates

In 1893 Katharine Bates took a vacation to the mountains of Colorado. She took a trip to the top of Pike's Peak and was so thrilled that she thought, "O beautiful for spacious skies." These few words became the beginning of the song "America the Beautiful." When Miss Bates returned from her trip, she finished writing her song.

The words to this song are full of hope and faith in God. It reminds us of the fact that God provides for all of our needs by His grace. Today, "America the

Beautiful" is one of the most awe-inspiring, best-loved songs. Ask your teacher to help you sing this song.

O beautiful for spacious skies,
    For amber waves of grain,
For purple mountain majesties,
    Above the fruited plain!
America! America!
    God shed His grace on thee
And crown thy good with brotherhood
From sea to shining sea!

O beautiful for pilgrim feet,
    Whose stern, impassioned stress
A thoroughfare for freedom beat
    Across the wilderness!
America! America!
    God mend thine every flaw,
Confirm thy soul in self-control,

    Thy liberty in law!

O beautiful for heroes proved
    In liberating strife,
Who more than self their country loved,
    And mercy more than life!
America! America!
    May God thy gold refine
Till all success be nobleness
    And every gain divine!

O beautiful for patriot dream
    That sees beyond the years
Thine alabaster cities gleam
    Undimmed by human tears!
America! America!
    God shed His grace on thee
And crown thy good with brotherhood
    From sea to shining sea!

Chapter 7 Review   4-20-16

Fill in the blanks with the correct answers.

1. The _____cotton gin_____ helped farmers clean their cotton quickly and cheaply so it could be sold to people who make clothes.

2. Mr. _____Edison_____ invented the electric light bulb.

3. The automobile was made quickly and cheaply by _____Henry T. Ford_____.

4. The invention of the steamboat made it possible for ships to travel without the _____wind_____.

5. The _____telegraph_____ and _____telephone_____ were inventions that helped Americans send messages to or talk with people far away.

6. The _____airplane_____ was invented by Orville and Wilbur Wright in 1903.

7. An _____immigrant_____ is a person who moves away from his own nation to set up his home in another land.

8. The United States government started to treat the _____Indians_____ honestly after the year 1900.

9. _____Bates_____ wrote the song "America the Beautiful."

Modern American cities often have big buildings called skyscrapers. Have you ever been up in a tall skyscraper?

8 America in Modern Times

> **Hear the word of the Lord, you children of Israel, for the Lord brings a charge against the inhabitants of the land: "There is no truth or mercy or knowledge of God in the land...."**
> **—Hosea 4:1**

Have you ever heard of a teddy bear? Did you know that it is named after one of our presidents, Theodore Roosevelt?

Keeping America Beautiful

President Roosevelt was often called "Teddy" by his friends. One day, when Mr. Roosevelt was out bear hunting with a few friends, he saw a small bear. He decided not to shoot the tiny animal because it was too small. Mr. Roosevelt was a wise hunter and kind Christian man. He knew that if too many small bears were killed, it would not be long before all the bears would be gone.

When Teddy's friends told newspaper writers about this bear story, an article soon appeared. People read this nice story about "Teddy's bear,"

Bears love to play in streams and hunt for fish.

and soon people were wanting to buy teddy bears for their children.

National parks are a great place to visit. Many Americans go to these parks on vacation or just to camp for the night.

President Roosevelt was not only interested in small bears. He was concerned that animals and human beings have enough forest lands and parks to explore for years to come. When Mr. Roosevelt became President of the United States in 1901, he came up with the idea of setting up huge "National Parks." The parks would be set up in many areas around the country, so all Americans would have a place to go camping, hiking, or hunting in God's wonderful creation.

So, thanks to the wise thinking of President Roosevelt, he was able to save little bears and big forests!

President Roosevelt was a fine leader who loved the great outdoors.

Help Keep America Beautiful

Write down three things that you can do to help keep America beautiful.

5-4-2016

1.	pick up trash when you see it.
2.	Not littering
3.	planting trees & flowers

Yellowstone National Park has many beautiful waterfalls.

Have you ever planted a tree? Ask your parent to help you plant your very own tree as a special project. Trees help to clean the air we breathe and make our land a beautiful place in which to live.

In modern times, our beautiful nation has become more difficult to keep clean because more people keep coming to the United States each year. Government leaders often have problems with people who pollute, or make a mess of, our nation's lakes and lands. Pollution, however, is not the only modern problem facing leaders in the United States. Our national or federal government, along with the state governments, help to make laws to try to solve problems.

Capital Cities

Each of the fifty states has its own capital city where its state leaders meet to make new laws or rules. These state governments are very important because the national government can only fix certain kinds of problems well. Americans believe that their state lawmakers can do a better job at fixing most problems because they know the needs of their local cities and people. State leaders, as well as local leaders in cities and towns, are more in touch with the people they live with than national government leaders who live far away.

The Government of the United States

1.	What state do you live in?
	Wisconsin
2.	What is the name of your state capital?
	Madison

■ Activity

1. Have your teacher show you a map of your local city and a map of your state. Can you see how much bigger a state is compared to a city?

2. Have your teacher show you a map of your country, the United States. Can you see how much bigger a country is compared to a city or state?

The President of the United States lives in the White House. Do you know the name of the President of the United States today?

Our national government has only one capital city, which is located in the District of Columbia. We call this capital city Washington, D.C.

Our President lives in the city of Washington. He is chosen by the people every four years. We call the President's home the White House. The first President to live in the White House was John Adams. He started living in the President's house in 1800. Americans visit the White House from time to time to see its great beauty. Have you ever visited the President's home?

Two other important buildings are found in Washington, D.C. They are known as the Capitol and the Supreme Court Buildings. The Capitol Building with its big

The Supreme Court Building

The Capitol Building

round dome is where leaders from all the fifty states meet to make laws for our country. Our national leaders, called representatives and senators, promise before God that they will only support and pass laws that are true to our Constitution.

The Supreme Court Building is the place where our most powerful judges work. These judges, who are chosen by the President, are given the job of protecting all Americans from unjust laws. The high Court has the responsibility to make sure that all state laws follow the Constitution of the United States.

Our Nation's Flag Today

As our nation has changed and grown over the years, our beloved flag has changed with it. The first American flag had thirteen stars on it. Since 1960 our country has had fifty stars on its flag—one star for each state in the Union. The stars are white and are on a blue background.

The American flag also has seven red stripes and six white stripes on it. The total number of stripes on the American flag remind us of when our nation first began with thirteen states. That is why our flag has thirteen stripes. The colors of our flag—red, white, and blue—stand for the following important things.

The red, white, and blue colors of the American flag stand for important Christian values.

1.	Red stands for courage.
2.	White stands for purity and liberty.
3.	Blue stands for faithfulness and loyalty.

Our flag is an important symbol of our nation's unity and love of liberty. Some people like to call our flag the "Stars and Stripes." Can you guess why this name is sometimes used?

American Soldiers Fight for Freedom

America had become a great nation because it was filled with hard-working people who loved God and their neighbors. Since the year 1900, America has often been called upon to help other nations or people who were fighting for their freedom. During the last one hundred years, the United States has become involved in six big wars. Two of these wars were so big that they were called "world wars." World War I (1914–1918) and World War II (1939–1945) were both fought around the world. The Korean War (1950–1953) and the Vietnam War (1964–1973) were both fought in small countries in Asia. The last war of the twentieth century was located in the Middle East and was called the Persian Gulf War (1991). Since the September 11, 2001, attacks on the United States, we have been fighting the Global War on Terror.

This monument honors the memory of all those who fought for freedom during World War II.

The Army

The Air Force

Thousands of brave Americans were killed in these wars. They gave their lives so that other people in the world might know the joy of being free. By helping to make people free, these fighting men lived out the command of Jesus to "Love your neighbor as yourself" (Matthew 22:39).

God has always been faithful to provide the United States with people who are willing to fight and die for freedom. We should be thankful to God for people who serve our nation in the army, the navy, the marines, or the air force. Christians should also pray for the Lord to protect and bless those who serve the holy cause of freedom.

The Navy

The Marine Corps

In recent years, new inventions keep changing the way that Americans live. The television, computer, and cell phone let people know what is happening around the world. Videos and computers help us to learn about many things while we have fun watching the programs. Computers also help many Americans as they work at their jobs.

Modern Inventions

The Cell Phone

The Television

The Laptop Computer

Neil Armstrong, an American, was the first man to walk on the moon.

One of the most exciting changes in modern America has been the space program. Starting in 1962, the American government began to build a spaceship that could take people to the moon and back. President John F. Kennedy said that the United States would put a man on the moon before the year 1970. By God's grace, the United States was able to put a man on the moon in 1969. Astronaut Neil Armstrong was the first person to ever walk on the moon.

Not all of the recent changes in America have been good. From the beginning of our nation, the people of the United States were not perfect. All people, including those who live in America, are sinners and sometimes do foolish things. One very foolish thing that many Americans did was to forget that God was the Giver of all good things, including freedom.

As the Lord began to bless the United States more and more, many people became very rich and proud during the 1900s. These foolish Americans began to say, "Look at what a great job we have done in making our country strong." They forgot that it was God's power that made us a strong nation.

Little by little, our nation began to turn away from God's Law. For many Americans, the only thing that they wanted to do was think about their own fun. The sin of pride turned many Americans into selfish people who no longer cared to love their neighbor or God. The Bible was taken out of our nation's schools, courts of law, and civil government rules. Prayer to God was no longer thought of as important to our nation or people.

Forgetting God is a big mistake, even for a strong nation like the United States. The Bible tells us, "Blessed is the nation whose God is the Lord" (Psalm 33:12). As America has turned away from God in recent years, Almighty God is slowly removing His blessings from our land. Our cities are filling up with groups of sad, poor, and hurting people. These sad people have forgotten how to love or be loved.

The Lord is using these problems to humble people and to take away their pride. More and more Americans are beginning to turn back to God. Christians are also beginning to wake up and see that they must take the light of God's Word into the whole world. Slowly but surely, God's people are once again beginning to reach out to hurting and sad people with the love of Christ.

Boys and girls in America today need to decide if they will serve God or serve themselves. The sooner girls and boys decide to walk in God's love, the sooner they will find the joy of having Jesus as their Savior, Helper, and Friend. The Lord has created you to help return our nation to Jesus Christ. You can be part of God's wonderful plan to heal our broken land by seeking Him in prayer.

If My people who are called by My name will humble themselves, and pray and seek My face, and turn from their wicked ways, then I will hear from heaven, and will forgive their sin and heal their land.
—2 Chronicles 7:14

Boys and girls can help to make the United States a strong and blessed nation by working hard. God wants young people to do the following things:

1.	Help your parents around the house and obey their rules. A hard-working and happy family will make the United States a strong nation.
2.	When you earn money, be sure to save some of it each month. God also wants you to give one dime out of every dollar you earn to your local church.
3.	The Lord wants you to use your time and money wisely. Do not spend your time or money on foolish things.

Have you ever asked yourself, "What will I become when I grow up?" The answer to this question is known only to God. Some will become firemen, carpenters, or preachers; others will become nurses, teachers, or homemakers. You can choose from thousands of possibilities open to you in America.

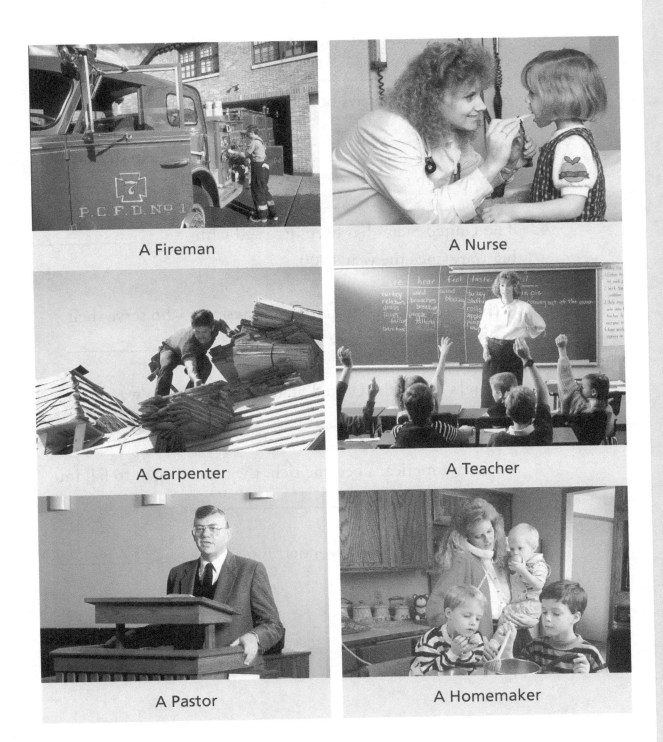

A Fireman

A Nurse

A Carpenter

A Teacher

A Pastor

A Homemaker

Chapter 8 Review

Fill in the blanks with the correct answers.

1. The _____ _____ was named after President Theodore Roosevelt.

2. President Theodore Roosevelt set up a program to start _____ so the people and animals of America would always be able to enjoy the forests.

3. Planting a _____ can help to clean the air we breathe.

4. The United States has been involved with _____ big wars since the year 1900.

5. We should be thankful to those Americans who serve their nation in the army, navy, marines, or _____.

6. By God's grace, the United States space program was able to put a man on the _____ in 1969.

7. As many Americans became rich, they soon began to fall into the sin of _____.

8. You are a part of God's wonderful plan to _____ our broken land.

9 America in the Days to Come

Trust in the Lord with all your heart, and lean not on your own understanding. In all your ways acknowledge Him, and He shall direct your paths.—Proverbs 3:5–6

The same God that made the world keeps it going day by day. He has a perfect plan for the United States and for all the nations of the world. God also has a plan for your life.

We are now at the end of our long trip through American history. Our story began with God's creation of men and nations. We then saw how the Lord used people like the Vikings and Christopher Columbus to open up the secret continents of North and South America. Then we studied the movements of explorers and settlers from Europe to the land of the American Indians. We hope you also remember how the thirteen English colonies sprang up and how the colonies grew into the United States of America.

The United States will be blessed as long as its people honor the Lord of heaven and earth. The Creator God is greater than a powerful spacecraft flying into outer space.

Our great country has a wonderful past. We hope that you have enjoyed learning the story of how the United States began and developed. However, you must now begin to think about the days ahead. The United States is not as good as it can be—far from it. As a young American, you will soon have to grow up and take part in the building of America. Ask the great Creator God to help you do your duty as a good soldier of Jesus Christ!

The road of life has many twists and turns, but God can make our way straight. God alone can guide us in the right paths.

Index

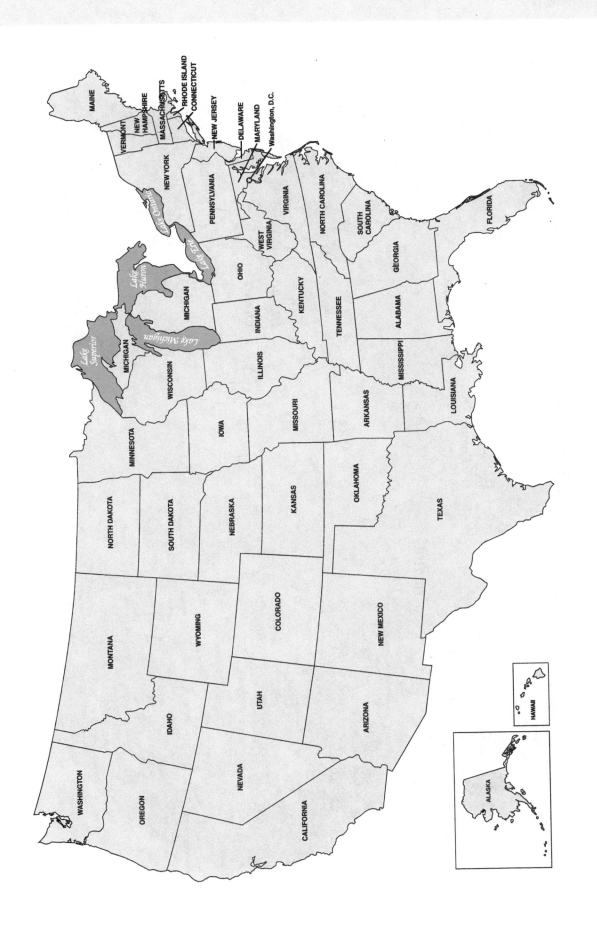

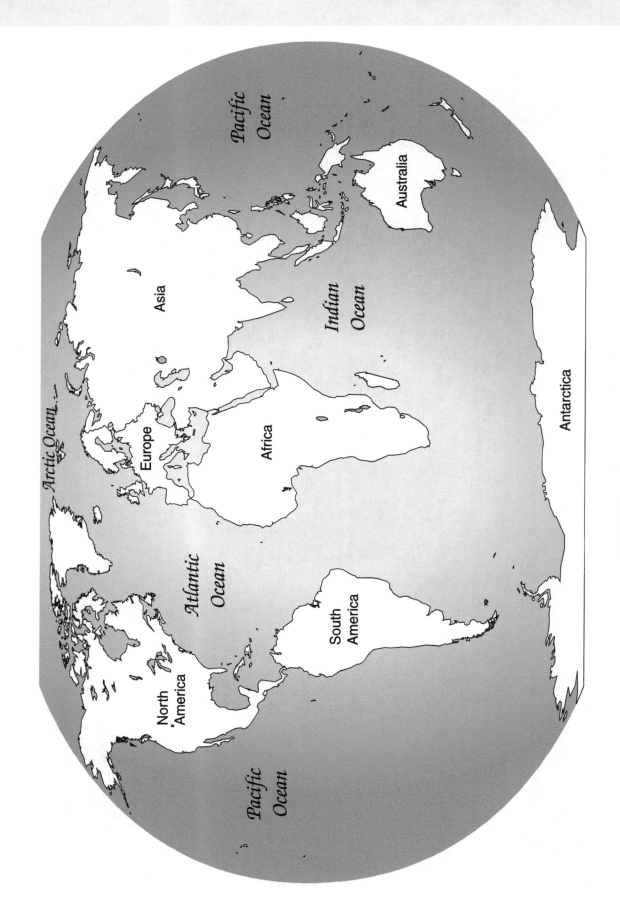